How to Start an Online Tutoring Business

Business

Making 4-5 Figures a Month

Joanne Kaminski

Table of Contents

Do You Need Help Getting Students? 7

Introduction... 9

Step I MINDSET 14

1 An Inside Peek at My Foundation and Early Belief Systems ...15

2 Five Failed Businesses...22

3 Mindset Changes 31

4 How Successful can a Tutoring Business Be? 41

5 How Much Does It Cost to Run an Online Tutoring Business? 50

Step 2 ORGANIZED SYSTEMS 63

6 Figuring out your Niche and your Ideal Client 64

7 Favorite Online Organizational tools you can't live without ..69

Step 3 MARKETING 79

8 Where Will I Get My Students?..80

9 Building Trust with Potential Online Clients 93

10 Testimonials...96

Step 4 SERVICES 104

11 Free Assessment and Free Report 105

12 Connecting with your students 115

13 Good Communication...120

14 Jumpstart Program 125

15 What Your Life Could Look Like......................................129

16 Now What?..135

ABOUT THE AUTHOR 137

Joanne Kaminski

ACKNOWLEDGMENTS

I want to acknowledge my fantastic team at the Online Tutor Coach. You always believe in me and keep me going. Without you, none of this would be possible.

Do You Need Help Getting Students?

This book contains some of the most effective tools that I have utilized to start my own tutoring company. Because I was once was where you are today, I want to give you the tool I wish I had when I started.

This tool is "50+ Ways to Get Online Tutoring Students". It is a workbook that will guide you in how to get those first students. Do you want to know the number one way that will work get students? We all do. Here is the thing. By trying many different things, you will begin to see the most helpful strategies for your tutoring business.

In this workbook, I have included a list of getting students and a strategy you can implement. You will use the strategy worksheet to keep track of the methods you have used and which ones you have not tried yet.

Then I have designed a marketing planner so that you can stay consistent with your efforts. Taking daily actions will be the secret to your success. I have even created a 30-day challenge to keep you going. My goal is to help you achieve your dreams with your tutoring business.

As a bonus, I have included "The Top 5 Mistakes that Tutors Make" so that you can avoid them. I am giving this to you free as my way of saying thank you for purchasing this book.

https://www.onlinetutorcoach.com/50-ways-to-get-online-tutoring-students

Joanne Kaminski

Introduction

The pandemic changed everything. In-person tutors were forced to stop tutoring or move online. Teachers were forced to find new ways to teach their students online through Zoom. To some, it felt like the world was crashing down on them. But for me, it was business as usual.

Instead of losing students, I gained students. Even with people losing their jobs, they sought out online tutoring services because they didn't want their children to get behind.

My days went from working 12:00 pm to 8:00 pm to 6:00 am to 8:00 pm. I was beyond booked solid because of the online presence that I had created before the pandemic started.

I began working weekends to help tutors with getting more students because there was nothing else to do. I figured that I might as well help others instead of staying cooped up in my house with nowhere to go.

Like everyone else, I thought the nationwide quarantine would last three weeks, but each week seemed to add another week or 2 or 3. Three months later and the situation was pretty much the same. Schools hoped to go back in person the next school year, and it kept feeling that the end was near.

You probably remember this as well. Many schools did a hybrid model, and some schools in states like New York and California stayed online the entire year. Virtual schooling caused a greater need for tutoring as students cut their video, hid behind a photo or black screen, and did other things.

Younger kids missed out on much-needed reading

instruction. I saw kids in 1st and 2nd grade who struggled more with reading foundations due to the previous year. Kids were scoring lower on the ACT and the SAT than they had ever scored before.

The pandemic caused many economic problems but also a substantial educational crisis. Kids who may never have needed a tutor needed one now more than ever.

There is no shortage of students to tutor, but there certainly is a shortage of people who can tutor them. Some say that I was ahead of the curve since I started in 2010. Some think these methods will decline as the pandemic gets behind us. I see an educational revolution opening up the world to learning online as it has never experienced before.

I have seen Zoom change to be more friendly for school systems and tutoring. New platforms are being designed to excite kids about learning online, like Koala. (I will share more about this incredible tool in the section about technology.) There are even platforms like Schoolified that make teaching groups of students a breeze.

The pandemic opened our eyes up to a need. The need is for our teaching styles to incorporate 21st-century technology. No longer do kids need to be taught by sitting at a desk. They can learn as an avatar in an online virtual world and have fun. Learning should be fun. Let's bring the joy back into our teaching so that kids want to learn.

I have found that joy with online tutoring. I have fallen in love with teaching again. So have the many people who have jumped on the bandwagon with me and feel the same way.

Kelly Michele, a tutor from Ontario, Canada, said, "*Yes! It actually has! I took this year off to find another career because I was*

DONE with teaching. I started tutoring just to make some money until I figured out what to do and guess what? I love tutoring! I've started my own business and I have big dreams in education again.

In the beginning, I had no idea how to turn this dream into a reality. Then one day, all of the answers started coming to me. I knew how it could work. I was so excited about turning this dream into a reality, but there was fear involved. I had to put that fear on the backburner while I made a go at it.

Many people each year try to make a go at this dream and don't get very far. They let some of the stumbling blocks become boulders and quit. They let fear stop them from accomplishing their dream. Voices inside their head tell them that this can't be done. People tell them that kids need in-person tutoring because online tutoring is impersonal and therefore ineffective. Those voices inside your head and those people are all wrong.

I have created systems to turn this dream into a reality for myself and you. I had to learn the hard way by digging my feet in, working hard, and doing a whole bunch of things wrong before I knew how to do them right.

Today I have a remarkable gift for you. You don't need to learn the hard way as I did. Follow me, and I will guide you in how to do it the easy way. I will share the 4-step system that I have used to make this an easy lifestyle. A lifestyle that allows me to bring my job with me anywhere in the world. A lifestyle that has enabled me to be a mom that is around to raise my children and live a lifestyle that is something way beyond anything that I could ever have dreamed.

I am not going to keep this 4-step system a secret. I am going to begin by sharing it with you right from the start. Then I will share my story with you and why I am qualified to teach you these systems. Next, I will give you tools to begin using to become an online tutor in any subject.

The 4-step system to being a profitable online tutor includes:

1. Mindset
2. Organized Systems
4. Powerful Marketing
5. Services

A different mindset is needed if you are considering online tutoring as a career choice. Online tutoring wasn't a career choice that even existed when we were kids.

Indeed, a different mindset is needed when it comes to how much money we can make. A different mindset is required, from having a job to a career to a business. A different mindset is needed to create your success.

To be successful, you need to have systems in place. A business that is not well thought out and not organized will fail. Tutoring businesses that are not organized put their chances in luck instead of what has been proven to work. They don't take the steps that they need to take to be successful. Being an online tutor requires these effective systems.

You do not need to be tech-savvy to do online tutoring. The tech you use can be as complicated or as easy as you would like. If you find that tech is not your thing, check out the tools I suggest to make it easier. Ready to learn more advanced tools, then I have you covered as well. I will rate each tool on level of difficulty so that you can determine which technology will be a good fit for you.

Online tutors need to have a powerful marketing strategy.

Many of the online tutors out there today just put themselves on lists that never get them found. This book will give you tools right out of the gate to get seen by the people you want to find you. People who get started in this career think that if they make a website, others will find them accidentally on the web. This idea is not accurate. You will learn powerful marketing strategies that will get you found and have more students than you can service independently. Wouldn't that be an excellent problem to have?

Lastly, you need to provide online services that deliver the result the client wants. If a child is struggling with reading, and you are a reading tutor, you need to increase their reading level. You will learn how to provide services that people want for their child. You will stand out amongst the crowd and become competition and recession-proof.

Online tutoring is projected to grow from a 6.57 billion a year industry[1] in the US in 2020 to 18.8 billion by 2028. As you know, children are being faced with higher standards every day. Higher standards mean more need for online tutoring than has ever been needed before. The pot is big enough for you to find the clientele you want to service and provide those services better than others out there.

Along with systems to run a tutoring business, you will get answers to the most frequently asked questions and solutions to frequent fears that people have. Some of those questions are, "How successful can an online tutoring business be?" Another one is, "Where will I get students?" The big one is about the bottom line. "How much will it cost me to start my own business as an online tutor and run it?"

This book will provide all of these answers and more. The only question left is, are you ready to dive in with me and take this journey?

Step I

MINDSET

1 An Inside Peek at My Foundation and Early Belief Systems

I was born and raised in a small town called Auburn, Massachusetts. Growing up, my dad was a machinist at a local manufacturing firm called ATF Davidson. He was making decent money, but the unionized workers went on strike often.

My mom stayed home and took care of me for a few years, but soon she found herself having to get a part-time job working at a restaurant close to home called Friendly's. Both of my parents worked hard and taught me all about a good work ethic. Their philosophy was, "Anything worth doing is worth doing well."

I did not realize growing up that this world consists of people with two different mindsets. There are the people who work their butts off for a small amount of money and those that seem to attract money quickly and efficiently. I grew up in a family that worked their butt off.

My mom instilled the value that whatever I do, I should do it well. I didn't always get the best grades, but my mom would always ask me if I tried my best when it came to school. When I told her that I did, she would say, "That is the only thing that I can ask of you." The good thing is that I knew that I would always make my mom happy no matter what I did or what I accomplished. I never felt like I had to prove my worth to her because I was perfect the way I was in her eyes.

We had very little money growing up. I would always see my dad or dad stressed out about it. Many fights in our household revolved around money, and I can only imagine their fears due to the lack of funds.

One day the company that my dad worked for closed down. He went from making decent money to making much less.

As a direct result, my mom got a full-time job at a car insurance company. She hated her job and complained every single day that she came home from work. She was not happy with the deck of cards that life seemed to have dealt her.

Every day when she went to work, she had the opportunity to talk to people who were in a car accident. They wanted to get money, and when my mom would have to say no, they would yell at her. So, all day long, she listened to people yell at her. Or, at least that was my understanding as a child.

I didn't want to take that path. I didn't want to work in a job that I hated. I didn't want to work at a job that didn't pay well. I knew from an early age that I would make more than enough money so I could do the things I desired.

I was programmed early on to get a job. My grandparents had jobs, my parents had jobs, and all my friend's parents had typical jobs. So, I always pictured myself getting a job. But not just any job; I was going to be a lawyer. I thought that was where all of the money was. One time a friend told me that she would be a lawyer, so I had figured that if she could be a lawyer, then so could I.

My dad supported this idea and thought that I would make a great lawyer. Every time we got into an argument, he told me that my arguing skills would come in very handy as a lawyer. I took this as a compliment and as fuel for keeping this dream alive to become a lawyer.

I began looking at schools to attend for college and other schools that had a promising law program. I chose Marquette University because I had heard they had an excellent pre-law program and a law school.

I was so excited about going to college and starting this chapter of my life. In my first year in college, I decided to join a group called the Mock Trial group. I had never been part of something like this before. I enjoyed the acting aspect.

However, there was one small problem that I found out about law that didn't fit my moral standards. When I learned that lawyers need to protect their clients even if they know their client is guilty, I realized this was not my career path.

I could not get over that sinking feeling I had deep in my heart that made me sick when I thought of it. When I thought about major crimes that people could have committed that they could get off of because of my skills as a lawyer, I realized that I did not want to continue on this path anymore. I treasured my morals, and you couldn't pay me enough money to put them on the back burner.

I had to reinvent my career path. I struggled with this process because ever since 6th grade, I had pretty much made up my mind about what I was going to do.

I remember one day walking on the Marquette campus between the Union and my dorm. I thought, "Hmmm, what is something that I am good at?" Then it came to me. I remember my mom saying that I was good with kids. So, I began to think about career paths that involved kids.

My desire to become a teacher was born that day. I remember when I told my parents that the expensive education they had worked their butt off to help me pay for was going to result in large dividends for them because I would become a teacher.

That was not a pleasant conversation. For the first time in my life, my parents were not happy about the decisions I was making. I think they had bought into this idea that I could become a lawyer. To go from a career path that could result in substantial money to working as a teacher was not their proudest moment for me.

In the school system, I put my work ethic in place. I was hired as a 3rd grade teacher at the Milwaukee Academy of Science. The goal was to infuse science into everything so that our school could promote scientists with diverse backgrounds. I loved the premise of this school.

It was a brand-new school in 2000, and I was a brand-new teacher. I put everything I could into my 3rd grade classroom. I would get there at 6:00 in the morning and not leave until 6:00 or 7:00 at night. I wanted to give the best to these kids.

I struggled with classroom management my first year, as many teachers do. I also experienced culture shock. While I grew up in poverty, I didn't understand the differences between white people's poverty and black people's poverty. Black people in the inner city had rules of survival that were unfamiliar to me.

It was a whole new world, and I got an education that first year far beyond what my students got. One thing that upset me deeply was that only 30% of our students were reading at grade level. My heart went out to these kids. I wanted to teach them grade-level content, but it is easier for them to mess around to avoid doing work when too many kids were reading at a kindergarten level.

In my second year of teaching 3rd grade, I began to dive into learning everything about teaching reading. It became an obsession for me. The principal noticed that I had this passion and asked if I would be interested in training to become a trainer for our reading program. I said yes and began training the Success for All reading program at Edison Schools all over the United States. I did this all while teaching 4th grade the following year. It meant writing lots of substitute lesson plans, but I didn't mind.

Then I became pregnant with my first child. By this time, I was training teachers and training the trainers of the SFA reading program. I knew that this lifestyle where I was traveling all over the country and teaching in the classroom would not be conducive to raising a family.

I decided the next year to leave the school I was at to be closer to home. As soon as I told the principal, she offered me the Reading Curriculum Coordinator position. I asked if I could change my hours slightly, and she said yes.

I left the classroom and began exploring the real challenges of raising the literacy rate in an inner-city school. At first, I was excited to be in the position. However, after several years I noticed a pattern.

Since we were in the inner city, we tended only to attract new teachers. These teachers came with the same struggles with classroom management that I had. Instead of sharing all of the knowledge I had learned about teaching reading, I spent most of my time helping them with classroom management.

Each year we had a 50% teacher turnover rate. I had no idea how to combat this, so I completed my master's and then decided to go to another school as a Reading Specialist.

Do you know how you think that if you were just at another school, then maybe things would be better? I had that thought. I left the Milwaukee Academy of Science and got a job closer to home in Waukesha. However, this new school was worse than the last one. It was so bad that I got sick and needed to take a leave of absence to take care of my health.

Once I came back, I sat in my chair in my office and had a revelation. The idea was, "I am not meant to be here." I had this sinking sensation because everything I had done had led me to this position. At first, I felt lost. I questioned my identity. If I am not a reading specialist, then who am I?

I knew that my family and my health needed to take the front seat. I decided I would leave the school system and figure out a way to work from home to be more present for my family.

Before I started with the Jumpstart program, I didn't have a structured system for my business, I didn't have good copy on my website, I wasn't confident in my ability to find students.

I learned a lot from Jumpstart, including how to effectively market my business, how to have sales conversations that convert, the systems I need to put in place to succeed (long-term) as a tutor, etc. I have really grown and become confident in myself as a tutor. I also believe that this is an endeavor that I can continue long-term.

Working with my coach Suzanne has been great. I have learned a lot from her. Partnering with other tutors and learning from them has been inspirational. And working with Joanne has been a blessing, she really offers good value for the investment.

Thank you Joanne Kaminski for your commitment to seeing other tutors succeed. I highly recommend tutors join the Jumpstart Masterclass because it will truly help them jumpstart their business or take their business to the next level.

Nana Nkrahene

Online Math Tutor

2 Five Failed Businesses

"Success is going from failure to failure without losing enthusiasm." – Winston Churchill

I would love to say that the first time I tried to run a business that I knew what I was doing and was successful right out of the gate. But that was not the case, and I consider myself a pretty intelligent person. My early failures are the whole reason I want to share systems with you that will help you start your business quickly and efficiently. If you have picked up this book, you are also a pretty intelligent person, and I don't want you to have to go through the learning curve that I did. I want to help speed up the process for you and make it as easy as possible, which is why I created the Jumpstart Your Online Tutoring Business Masterclass that you will learn about in chapter 14.

The first business that I failed at was trying to make money on eBay. Specifically, I sold used clothing that was in excellent condition. I sold the clothing in lots, thinking this would make it more valuable. With all of the shipping costs, this endeavor landed me in the hole. I had tried to read all of the books out there that would help me launch this successfully, but honestly, I think the whole eBay craze, which might have been profitable for small business owners like me at one time, was beginning to lose its steam. I tried learning from successful people, but I couldn't compete with all of the brick-

and-mortar companies that were selling their stuff dirt cheap to get it out of their inventory.

The next business that I began was called Leveled Literacy Intervention.[2] I had to sell the program, which taught people how to start their own company and sell tickets to conferences. In the entire six months that I was part of this venture, I spent a ton of money and sold only one $1,000 product. I did learn that I wanted to be passionate about whatever company I started. I also learned how to effectively talk to potential clients on the phone, centered on them and not on me.

My target clients were teachers like myself. They either wanted to leave the school system or were let go from the school system and were looking for a way to make money tutoring online. It stuck out to me that there was a need, but I couldn't provide that need for them at that time. My company didn't fit their need, so I would always end up wishing them luck as they pursued their future endeavors.

So far, this whole starting my own business thing was not working out quite like I thought that it would. The fear and frustrations that my husband was having seeing me not making a reliable income caused some resistance, hoping for success to come quickly and effortlessly my way. We feared not having enough money to pay off our bills and kept going into the negative and hitting our savings. The money situation wasn't looking good.

Then I remembered the program that I had that taught me how to run my own company. By this point, I was now able to create a website, do video marketing and get search engine optimization (SEO) results on page one of Google. I had this brand-new idea that I was excited to implement. This idea would help increase kids' reading levels while everyone got to have a good time. I thought I would sell vacations that the entire family could go on. There would be times when mom and dad could spend some alone time together while the kids read about the places they were visiting. Then they would have hands-on experiences at these exotic locations like Alaska and increase their background knowledge, which would increase their non-fiction reading levels.

I was excited to travel the world and increase kids' reading levels. It felt like a win-win. The only problem is that there was not a need for this. Nobody goes into Google and types "learning vacation". I had people tell me that vacations should be when kids get to relax, not learn. Every single negative thought that went through people's minds about this idea came out of their mouths. Or, so I thought.

In the end, this was not a service designed to solve problems for people. Thank goodness this didn't cost me anything. I didn't have to invest anything except for time. Unfortunately, Bright IDEA Vacations, where you get to discover, explore and have a reading adventure was never born.

I had always wanted to teach kids how to read online. Before I left my first teaching job, I mentioned this to one of my college professors, and she looked at me like I was crazy. She didn't see how I could effectively teach kids to read online, and her face backed that up. I had no idea how to make it work either. So, I began looking for an online teaching company that would hire me.

I found company after company that offered math, SAT, and ACT tutoring. Some companies offered language arts tutoring but not online tutoring for struggling readers. I honestly never had a desire to teach those other areas, so I left the dream of teaching online for a goal in the future.

I began to think about some other ways that I could make money. I felt that I could take my craft skills and start making money selling handmade jewelry on Etsy. I didn't sell one piece of jewelry online, so I decided to take my jewelry to a craft fair, get a table and sell it there.

Since the fair I was going to enter already had a ton of jewelry crafters, I knew I had to market with a novel focus. I made matching jewelry sets for little girls and their American Girl Dolls.

Do you think I was effective at this? Nope, women like to buy jewelry for themselves, but not so much for their little girls or their dolls. Also, on the day of the fair a disastrous hailstorm kept people home so instead of having 1,000 people walk through the door that day, only 200 people attended the event. I had set up my booth so that kids could color while the parents looked around. The only sale I made that day was a pity sale from a little girl that hung out with me coloring.

Making jewelry was another business venture that landed me into a negative profit. I spent about $300 on beads, $40 on a table, and made a whopping $10 from the event. Hmmm… I began to second guess my ability to start a successful business for myself and continued to brainstorm.

I remember going to an Usborne Book Party once, and I loved the books so much that I thought this was something that I could easily do. Anyone who knows me knows my passion for books, so this seemed like a no-brainer. I attended all of the trainings online, researched, purchased the start-up package, and had my open house. I was able to book parties from this, and my friends supported me in this venture.

The problem came when I ran out of friends. My friends were willing to have a party and support me, and even some of their friends booked parties, but after that, people just didn't want to have parties. It is a lot of work for people to bring a salesperson to their home to have a party, and people don't want to go through the effort of cleaning their house, inviting their friends, and having someone sell to them. Sometimes the perks were good enough for people to want to do this, but most people didn't want to invest their hard-earned dollars in what seemed to them as expensive but high-quality books. eBooks seemed to be taking off then, and if you can buy a book for .99 or $2.99, then the odds go down that you will buy them at full price and only read them once.

So, there you have it—five failed businesses and no real potential of earning an income. You may be wondering why I even chose to share that story with you. Well, I share it more because of what I have learned in starting my businesses than to tell you what a failure I have been in the past.

Through each of these businesses, I have learned that people don't care about the product you have to sell them. The only thing that people care about is what's in it for them. That is the only thing that will get people to part with their hard-earned dollars. As you start your own tutoring business, never think of it as a way to earn money and freedom for yourself, but honestly, think how can you be of service to your potential client. Remember that one thing that my mom taught me. "Whatever you do, do your best."

Here's another powerful thing that I learned through this process. If people's pain is great enough, they will pay for a solution. My first company on eBay did not solve any pain for anybody. People can find clothing anywhere. They can go to a rummage sale or Goodwill if money is short, but their pain is not great enough. The pain factor in your child falling behind in education is much greater. Parents' love for their children drives their need to resolve this pain.

26

In my second business, I learned that many people want to have financial freedom, but if something sounds too good to be true, they will put their guard up. When I ran my business with Etsy, I learned that you can't just put something on the internet anymore and expect people to find it. People don't find things on the internet by accident anymore. People and services get found because they have either done their research on SEO to create #1 rankings on Google, have paid for their rankings to show up as #1 and paid a ton of money, or have paid for someone who knows what they are doing in internet marketing.

The days of people finding you by accident are long over. Everything is very methodical. I will teach you what I have learned to do to get first page rankings. It won't happen overnight, but through time it will be possible. If you want to get started right now, then I suggest that you turn to Chapter 15. One of the subjects I teach in the Jumpstart Your Online Tutoring Business Masterclass is how to get first page search results on Google.

I learned from my venture with Bright IDEA Vacations that sometimes my ideas are not so bright. If you can't laugh at yourself, then who can you laugh at? Don't take yourself so seriously. Brush it off and find another way to turn your dreams into a reality.

I also learned that if my business is more of a benefit to me than for my clients, it will not be an effective business. People prosper in business because their services or products are something that other people need, not something I think they should need or want.

From Usborne Books, I learned that I don't enjoy selling low price products. If someone only buys one, then you don't make much of a profit. I have seen people buy one piece of jewelry from Silpada for $100 and seen both people walk away happy from the transaction. When I would sell my books, and someone bought one for $10, only one person walked away happy from that transaction, the customer. Selling books made me take stock of what my time is worth. In my tutoring company, I want my customers to feel that they are getting great value for their money, and I also need to be able to support my family so that I don't have to go out and get another typical job.

To sum up, I have learned the following from my businesses.

MINDSET
- We deserve to get paid for what we are worth for the time that we put in.
- Don't take yourself too seriously.
- Have fun with whatever business venture you decide to do. If it's not fun, then you are not doing it right.
- You can be, do, and have whatever your heart desires.

SYSTEMS
- Always get the training that you need and learn from others when you need it. Effective systems are within reach, especially with the Jumpstart Program.
- Don't reinvent the wheel. You will most likely fail unless you have an infinite amount of persistence.
- Learn effective systems from people that are more successful than you.

MARKETING

- People will not find you on the internet by accident.
- Your friends can only take you so far; you have to network and get yourself out there.
- Test your ideas out on others; they will let you know if you have a bright idea.

SERVICES

- Be of service to others.
- Address their pain and solve one of their problems.

This book is split up into these four categories because I believe this four-step system is the key to a successful online business. For those who want to travel this journey with others, I created the Jumpstart program. There I go into detail and support online tutors to become successful business owners who have financial freedom, flexibility, and a life beyond their wildest dreams.

People often ask me what the difference is between the Jumpstart Program and this book. I'll answer that for you. This book gives you an outline and resources to get your business up and running. The Jumpstart Your Online Tutoring Business Masterclass holds your hand through the entire process. There I provide opportunities to get your questions answered, network with other tutors, and grow your empire as big as you want to grow it.

Videos show you how to do each of the things we discuss in this book, along with tons of other valuable strategies. It is one thing for someone to tell you something, but it makes a world of difference when they show it to you.

Before I started the Jumpstart program, I had one student and I was tutoring for free. I was nervous about asking for the rate I wanted.

Then after I took the program, I suddenly started getting clients. This was mainly from learning how to do an effective flyer and to sign up for google my business. Each week the content was exactly what I needed. It was serendipitous.

A great thing about the program is having one or more accountability partners. You make great friends and connections. All of Joanne's content is amazing and so helpful. I could never have done this on my own.

-Justine Forelli

Online Reading Tutor

3 Mindset Changes

"You won't know the power of the journey until you step up each rung of the ladder toward what you want. Then, even if you get to the top and find this dream is no longer desirable, you will be viewing life from a higher vantage point and you will have grown in your ability to chase your own dreams." – Troy Fontana

As you can see, I didn't go to school to start my own business. It wasn't something that I even had considered before due to beliefs that were instilled in me. To go from a typical job to owning my own company, I had to go through an incredible mindset shift. I don't think any of this would have been possible without this mindset shift. Wayne Dyer wrote a book that goes into depth about this shift called, <u>The Shift: Taking your Life from Ambition to Meaning</u>[3].

At any time, even if you are part of a union, you can get let go. Often we think that a job is the safer route or more secure. When I had a job in the school system, I would constantly fear losing my job. This is not security. Growing up during the recession of the '80s taught me that there is no job security in a typical job where you get paid by an employer. This creates fear, stress, and hard times.

Stress from jobs was all I knew as a child. Since that was all I knew, I followed in the steps of my family and continued to get job after job after job. I didn't know any other way until I began to immerse myself with self-development material.

The Secret by Rhonda Byrnes[4] started to get me to think of making money in different ways that would support the lifestyle that I wanted to have. First, I had to figure out what lifestyle that was. I had to figure out what lifestyle I thought I deserved.

In the beginning, I thought that as long as I had a house, a family, and a career that I would be happy. Well, I had all of those things, and they didn't make me happy. After reading The Secret, I began visualizing my dream life. Since I was still teaching in the school system, I didn't see how this could be my reality, but I began to believe that I deserved it.

At the same time, I also began having a relationship with my Higher Power. I began to receive guidance in what I was meant to do, and I began to follow the calling of leaving the school system and starting something new.

In the book How to Make Great Things Happen in Your Life by Fred Schafer,[5] he mentions a study done at Yale University in 1959. All of the students were asked to answer a survey at the end of the year. The survey included the following question.

Do you have a precise written specification – a written focus- of how you want your life to be in 10 years? It would include a professional goal, relationship goal, and an overall goal in all areas of your life.

How many students do you think had these kinds of goals exiting one of the top universities in existence? If you guessed 3%, then you are correct. However, what I find even more astounding than that is ten years later, every single one of those students was contacted, and the results they found were staggering. The 3% that had clear, focused goals had achieved more happiness, obtained more tangible goals, created a sense of purpose in life, and they had accumulated more wealth than the remaining 97%.

People who don't make plans continue letting life determine their next step and going through the daily grind. Not many people enjoy the daily grind. I know that I didn't. I remember how I felt every Sunday night before I would have to go to work the next day. I would feel sick to my stomach.

Maybe tutoring isn't suitable for you; perhaps it's not your dream. Everyone's dream is going to be different, and that is okay. Do yourself a favor and write down what your five-year plan and ten-year plan are.

A mindset shift has to happen to go from being an employee to a small business owner. Some people don't want to be a business owner, but what if starting a solopreneur company like tutoring lets you have freedoms you didn't even know that you wanted? Would you be interested in making the shift?

For me it is so exciting not to go job from job to job anymore. Imagine having multiple streams of income versus just one stream of income. Many people have a lot of stress about losing their job because they don't know how to pay the bills if they lose their job. Their one source of making money is gone. Now what?

Today I have multiple streams of income coming in. There's tutoring, book sales, product sales, and subscriptions from my die-hard members of the Insider Secrets Group for Online Tutors. If one of these areas tanked, I wouldn't have to worry about making money. As each day goes on, money flows quickly and effortlessly into my bank account. Making money doesn't have to be hard anymore.

These thoughts have changed my mindset. Going from only making money on a job to having multiple income streams alleviates the stress involved with losing a job. One's mindset can go from a troubled world to a world where there is a solution around every corner, waiting to be found. Over the next couple of pages, you will see some activities that you can do to begin making mindset changes for yourself. These are not only empowering, but uplifting as well.

READ FOR AN HOUR A DAY

Before I even read the book <u>The Secret</u>, by Rhonda Byrnes[6] I did a program called "Tools to Life" by Coach Devlyn Steele. It was a free online program that was also pivotal in changing my mindset. It no longer exists, but it was incredible.

He gave a powerful suggestion to read every day for an hour. He challenges us to turn off the television 30 minutes before you go to bed and read instead. His reason is that we tend to listen to the news and it is filled with negative thoughts. If this is going on before we go to bed, then this is what travels through our brain throughout the night and the next day.

On top of reading for 30 minutes before you go to bed, he also suggests reading for an hour a day about things in your specific field. He says that if you do this every day for 3 years, by the end of that time, you will be an expert in your field.

Some of us go through the grind each day, and we don't feel we have the mental capacity to challenge our brains or read. It is so much easier to turn on the television. But honestly once you take on this challenge, you won't miss television one bit and you will feel like you are being more productive.

POSITIVE THOUGHTS VS. NEGATIVE THOUGHTS

Did you know that 60,000 thoughts that go through our brains every single day? About 80% of those thoughts are negative for most people according to Marci Shimoff[7]. Thinking 48,000 negative thoughts makes it hard to be grateful, but this is part of the mindset change.

S.L. Parker, in the book <u>212° The Extra Degree</u>[8], says this.

At 211 degrees, water is hot.
At 212 degrees, it boils.
And with boiling water, comes steam.
And with steam, you can power a train

Applying one extra degree of temperature to water means the difference between something that is simply very hot and something that generates enough force to power a machine.

The book also mentions that once your negative thoughts are at 49% and your positive thoughts are at 51% that you have reached this extra degree. You are now thinking more positively than negatively and can begin achieving the things that you want to achieve in your life.

GRATITUDE

Gratitude can be a tool to reach this 51%. Here is the quickest way to begin changing negative thoughts in positive thoughts.

1. Each morning when you wake up write down 5 things that you are grateful for.

2. Each morning before you go to bed write down 5 different things that you are grateful for.

It is easy to fall in a rut of saying the same things over and over again. So, if you make it a point to not repeat ones you have already thought of, you will begin training your brain to look for the positive instead of looking for the negative.

People have said that once they began doing this activity that their thoughts started to focus more on the positive and that they felt more excited to wake up in the morning. Gratitude is a game changer, and it is that one degree change that can make all of the difference.

SURROUND YOURSELF WITH TOP EXPERTS AND MOTIVATIONAL SPEAKERS

One thing that you can begin reading are books that begin to change your mindset from those negative thoughts to positive thoughts. A great resource to use is TED Talks online[9]. You will be introduced to amazing motivational speakers who have already had these mindset shifts.

Here are some of my favorite authors and the books that they have written.

Rhonda Byrnes – The Secret[10]

Wayne Dyer – Wishes Fulfilled: Mastering the Art of Manifesting[11]

Napoleon Hill – <u>Think and Grow Rich</u>[12]

Stephen Covey- <u>Seven Habits of Highly Effective People</u>[13]

Robert Kiyosaki – <u>Rich Dad, Poor Dad: What the Rich Teach their Children and the Poor and Middle Class Do Not!</u>[14]

Eckhart Tolle – <u>The Power of Now</u>[15]

Darren Hardy – <u>The Compound Effect</u> (Hardy, 2020)[16]

Esther Hicks – <u>The Law of Attraction</u>[17]

Jack Canfield – <u>Chicken Soup for the Soul: Think Positive</u>[18]

DECLUTTERING

So far, we have looked at negative thoughts and positive thoughts. Think about how surrounding yourself in things that you don't need or use has the ability to cause negative thoughts. More stuff means more cleaning and maintenance. Sometimes the stuff can take over. It takes over in the car, in the house, our office, and everywhere.

We know we should take action, but sometimes we spend more time thinking about how much we don't want to do it than it would take to do it.

I fell into this trap, but found an amazing resource called FlyLady[19] online. FlyLady gave me the tools I needed to turn my home into a place I love. What I have found is that when you surround yourself in things that you love, you take care of them more. Also, it brings you closer to the most powerful tool according Rhonda Byrnes in <u>The Power</u>[20]. That power is love. When you are in a mode of love you accomplish more.

You are inspired to take the actions in your life that you feel are necessary to take.

Decluttering your space is an amazing way to begin changing your environment and your mindset. Getting rid of the stuff in your life that you don't need, use, or love reduces a mental burden, and inspires you to conquer the next challenge.

VISUALIZATION

One of the most amazing tools you can utilize is the tool of visualization. Visualization allows you to think big and focus on what you want to attract into your life.

In some respects, our brains don't distinguish between what we experience and what we imagine. We can turn goals into things we know we can do when we fill out images in our minds so that they are as vivid as something we have already done. The key to visualization is believing what you are visualizing. If you can't believe you can attract what you are visualizing, then you won't bring it into your life.

Visualization can be done in several ways. Let's take a look at a couple of them.

First, you can visualize by closing your eyes and thinking about what you want to draw into your life. Allow your brain to go free and imagine having it. Next, focus on how it feels to have attracted that into your life. When you connect the feeling of love to what you want to attract, you are able to attract it quicker.

Another way to visualize is through using a dream board. You can collect images of the things that you want to attract into your life and put them on the dream board. Each day when you wake up you then focus on it and feel appreciation for attracting these things into your life.

I utilize this same concept on my computer. I take an image and set it as my background image. This allows me to focus on that one big dream that I want to attract. Every single time the big dreams have always come into my life.

In the next couple of chapters I am going to answer a few questions most people have about running their own online tutoring company. If this is your dream, you can visualize it and think big. Small business owners that think small don't attract big results. So, let's take a closer look at how successful a tutoring business can be and how much it costs to get started.

ACTION STEPS

1. Read an hour a day.

2. Write down 5 thing you are grateful for daily.

3. Read a personal development book.

4. Declutter your home and your surroundings.

5. Visualize what you want your life to be.

Before enrolling, my process for onboarding students involved a phone call or text, a trial session, and a follow-up email. Now, I am communicating value and professionalism far more effectively through using an assessment with detailed information and questions in the follow-up calls. By using this process, I have become far more confident about the price I charge and the value I provide.

Last week, for instance, I had someone tell me my rate was too expensive. Instead of moving on, I became curious and asked her what she was comparing my price to. When she answered, I explained why I charge the rate I do. I focused on communicating my value in a non-salesy way, rather than providing a discount. She became my client this week. This is the first time this has happened. And I know the shift in my approach has come from the insight and confidence gained in the course.

In the program, I onboarded 11 students (13 hours). This was a huge blessing during the summer. Thank you so much, Joanne.

Dustin Stevens,

Online Writing Tutor

4 How Successful can a Tutoring Business Be?

"Success is not the key to happiness. Happiness is the key to success. If you love what you are doing, you will be successful."   Herman Cain

When I first began thinking about running my own tutoring business, I wondered how successful this could be. The answer to this question is, your tutoring business can be infinitely successful if you change your mindset from seeing obstacles as roadblocks to seeing obstacles as opportunities.

To be completely honest with you, I didn't know in the beginning that my tutoring business was going to be as successful as it is. In fact, I started off teaching kids to read online for free because I did not even know if the tools I was putting in place were going to work.

In the beginning, I received a lot of resistance from parents who didn't trust Skype. Today I use Zoom, but I just need a reliable meeting tool so my students can follow my lead. I work with kids as young as 5 years old, and in some cases even 4-year-olds. Once I show parents how easy this is with

Zoom, they are hooked.

The best part is that I am able to get people to pay me top dollar for my services. At first, I was thinking that people might be willing to pay me at least what they would pay to other tutoring companies. After all, I was a certified reading tutor and reading specialist. I knew my services would be more convenient for the average busy family.

I found out that parents pay $40 per hour and up for the services that I provide. So, I started there. Right away, people were willing to pay this because they couldn't get these services cheaper anywhere else. Also, their child would be receiving top-notch one-on-one services, rather than sharing a tutor with a small group. I figured that I could raise the price as time went on, as demand for my services grew.

Guess what? I did. Once I got booked solid at $40 an hour, then I raised my rates to $50 an hour. After that $60, then $75. Today I charge $100 for my tutoring services. I take on fewer students because I also help tutors with starting, growing, and taking their tutoring business to the next level.

I work with my students for just one hour a week. Again, this is something that you can adapt to what works for you, but I found that two 30-minute sessions a week was a magic formula for younger kids. The kids didn't have to invest a ton of their time or get bored with a long session. More can get accomplished when you are able to split the hour. Brick-and-mortar companies have to do hour sessions to make their schedules work. I, on the other hand, can be accommodating to the students and their parents.

What a selling point! The parent does not need to go

anywhere to have their child tutored. This means that the parent can do one of the many other things that they need to accomplish such as laundry, dinner, exercise, or sit back and relax for a few minutes. Amazing!

Brick-and-mortar companies tend to have kids come in more than once a week. I have even heard of kids that had to come in 5 days a week for a full hour session. Wow, talk about making the kid hate learning!

What kid wants to spend their free time doing that? I had one client tell me how she couldn't have her daughter take part in any other activities because they had to drive an hour a day to the sessions and then stay for the hour. There just was no time for anything else. Online tutoring frees people to develop a well-rounded child and put time into their education. Now kids who receive tutoring can take part in sports that once were only a dream.

The nagging question you may be wondering is whether tutoring online can be profitable to you. Let's look at that. We are just going to stick with the $40 number since people are more than willing to pay this for your services. Of course, the more specified your niche, the more you can charge. We will also stick with the formula of tutoring for an hour a week. If you want to keep your teaching job and just work an extra 10 hours a week, then here is what that would look like.

10 hours x $40 = $400 extra a week = $1,600 extra a month

Wow, so if you work just ten hours a week, then you can make an extra $1,600 a month. What would your life look like if you were able to earn and extra $1,600 a month? Write it here.

What are some things that you would be able to do?

_____
_____
_____
_____

What are some things that you would be able to have?

_____
_____
_____
_____

Where are some places that you would get to travel?

_____
_____
_____
_____

Let's say that you just want to work during the summer. But you don't want to work full time because you have had a rough year. You would be happy with working just 20 hours a week. Right?

20 hours x $40 = $800 a week = $3,200 a month = $6,400 for a 2-month summer; or $9,600 for a 3-month summer

I am going to pose the same questions as before because I want you to think about how this can impact you.

What are some things that you would be able to do?

_____
_____
_____
_____

What are some things that you would be able to have?

_____

_____

_____

Where are some places that you would get to travel?

_____

_____

_____

_____

Let's say that you just want to work part time and have time to take care of your family. Maybe you want to be home for your own kids or maybe you want to watch your grandkids during the day. If you decided that you wanted to work 20 hours a week to have that balance, here is what the numbers would look like.

20 hours x $40 = $800 a week = $3,200 a month = $38,400 a year

So, you could bring in $3,200 a month working part time from your home. Wow, that is amazing. The best part is you can make this income and still do what you love to do, which is teach. What part time job can you get where you will work out of your home, not have to commute, not have a boss looking over your shoulder and make $38,400 a year?

What are some things that you would be able to do?

_____

_____

_____

What are some things that you would be able to have?

_____

Where are some places that you would get to travel?

_____

_____

Now some of you may be thinking, that just sounds way too good to be true. You may even be one of those people that has been wired to think that if it sounds too good to be true, then it is. I certainly was raised that way. I had to change that mindset into believing bigger than I ever envisioned before.

And just to show you that I am not making up these numbers and they are not theoretical, I have been working part time doing this for years. Here in figure 5.1 is what flowed into my PayPal account in January 2013, a short way in. I make even more today.

	Date	Type	Name/Email	Payment status	Details	Order status/Actions	Gross	Fee	Net amount
	Jan 30, 2013	Recurring Payment From	Tammy Belshaw	Completed	Details	Issue refund	$160.00	-$4.94	$155.06 USD
	Jan 28, 2013	Recurring Payment From	Nancy Barth	Completed	Details	Issue refund	$27.00	-$1.08	$25.92 USD
	Jan 28, 2013	Payment From	Mark Lovie	Completed	Details	Issue refund	$600.00	-$23.70	$576.30 USD
	Jan 25, 2013	Recurring Payment From	Andrew McIntyre	Completed	Details	Issue refund	$80.00	-$2.62	$77.38 USD
	Jan 24, 2013	Payment From	Grace Engel	Cleared	Details	Print shipping label ▾	$20.00	-$0.88	$19.12 USD
	Jan 20, 2013	Payment From	Susan Butkus	Completed	Details	Issue refund	$80.00	-$2.62	$77.38 USD
	Jan 16, 2013	Payment From	Grace Engel	Cleared	Details	Issue refund	$20.00	-$0.88	$19.12 USD
	Jan 16, 2013	Payment From	Andrea Wood	Completed	Details	Issue refund	$1,400.00	-$54.90	$1,345.10 USD
	Jan 15, 2013	Payment From	Christopher Toy	Completed	Details	Issue refund	$180.00	-$5.52	$174.48 USD
	Jan 13, 2013	Payment From	Charles Tellis	Completed	Details	Issue refund	$160.00	-$4.94	$155.06 USD
	Jan 10, 2013	Payment From	shari dempski	Completed	Details	Issue refund	$80.00	-$2.62	$77.38 USD
	Jan 10, 2013	Payment From	Grace Engel	Cleared	Details	Print shipping label ▾	$20.00	-$0.88	$19.12 USD
	Jan 7, 2013	Payment From	Andrea Wood	Completed	Details	Issue refund	$240.00	-$9.66	$230.34 USD
	Jan 6, 2013	Payment From	Rebecca Tiongson	Completed	Details	Issue refund	$160.00	-$4.94	$155.06 USD
	Jan 1, 2013	Payment From	Sarah Thusius	Completed	Details	Issue refund	$160.00	-$4.94	$155.06 USD

$3,261.00

figure 5.1

During this month I brought in $3,261.00 and I was only

working 11 hours a week.

We started off talking about some pretty small numbers because I wanted you to see how even doing this a few hours a month can impact your income. Now let's take a look at someone who is serious about making this a full-time career.

40 hours x $40 = $1,600 a week =$6,400 a month = $76,800 a year

How many teachers do you know that are making $76,000 a year? That is an end of your career salary for most regions. You can begin making this today and this is just when you start out. Remember how I mentioned that supply and demand can dictate that you can charge more? Well, let's take a look at how the numbers change as soon as you start charging $50 an hour.

40 hours x $60 = $2,400 a week = $9,600 a month = $113,200 a year

Do you know any classroom teachers that are making this? The answer is no. That pay scale doesn't exist. Teachers have never been able to make a 6-figure income in my area. With your own online tutoring company, you can. I do all of this without the stress of the administration breathing down my neck, telling me what to do, when to do it, and how to do it. I want you to think bigger than you have ever been able to think before. What would your life look like if you were making $113,200 a year?

What are some things that you would be able to do?
_____
_____
_____
_____

What are some things that you would be able to have?

_____

_____

_____

_____

Where are some places that you would get to travel?

_____

_____

_____

_____

People will pay you what you are worth if you carry yourself professionally and charge a price that reflects the value of your time. Not only get to be the owner of your life, with the flexibility that you may have always desired, but you also get to be the owner of your very own business. Honestly, what is possible is going to be completely up to you. I will share with you all of the tips and tricks that I use to run my business if you stick with me long enough. You will learn how to do this and find the people that want to hire you for your services.

I am amazed at how quickly I have gone from charging $14 an hour in 2017 to $100 an hour in 2021 with the help of Joanne and her programs.

Allen Tsao

Online Math Tutor

5 How Much Does It Cost to Run an Online Tutoring Business?

The next question that may be going through your mind, now that you have an idea of what you can earn is how much will running my own tutoring business cost me? With internet advancements, running an online tutoring business has never been easier. In the past if someone wanted to purchase a franchise and run a tutoring business, he or she would have to find a brick-and-mortar building and pay rent each month.

I went online to research how much it would cost to start a franchise with one of the big tutoring companies. The names of those companies are left out, but I share this information here to put into perspective how creating your own online tutoring business gives you tremendous advantages.

In order to own a franchise, you will have to attend formal training on their business operations, methods, and programs. You will pay for that training, both initially and ongoing. Don't forget the cost of the franchise itself.

Usually, the brick-and-mortar space requires changes to get permitted and to effectively run your business. Those can cost up to $9,000 just for the architect. The actual improvements can cost between $30,000 and $60,000.

Once the building is secured and renovated to meet your needs, you then need to furnish the building. That costs anywhere between $10,000 and $20,000. A good computer is also essential and will cost from $800 to $1,500.

Are you getting tired yet, with all of these numbers and the costs involved? It seems astronomical to me. This is only the tip of the iceberg. Each month you need to pay your employee payroll and each month you need to pay about $1,500 in rent. Don't forget about ongoing costs like electricity and water.

I have listed all of the costs in Figure 8.1. The overall cost of running your very own tutoring franchise can be anywhere from $81,243 to $157,750 in the first 3 months. I don't know about you, but I don't even know how to get ahold of that kind of money.

Resources	Low Cost	High Cost
Training Agreement Deposit Fee	$500	$500
Expenses while training	$3,945	$5,460
Initial Franchise Fee	$1,000	$1,000
Initial purchase of materials	$1,000	$1,000
Architect design	$0	$9,000
Leasehold improvements	$30,000	$60,000
Furniture, signs, equipment, supplies	$10,000	$20,000
Notebook computer at center	$800	$1,500
Professional fees	$1,000	$3,000
Liability insurance	$400	$400
Business license, name registration	$100	$200
Lead management system	$340	$340
Recommended reading list	$2,240	$2,290

Fingerprinting, criminal background check	$18	$60
Rent	$1,500	$4,000
New center marketing	$2,000	$5,000
Payroll cost for assistants	$14,400	$20,000
Utilities	$12,000	$24,000
Total	**$81,243**	**$157,750**

Figure 8.1

When I take a look at these numbers, I realize how truly lucky I am to have the lifestyle that I have. Never before has owning your own tutoring business been easier. Would you like to know the total cost for me to get my business started? I spent $0. I didn't have to invest one penny to get started. I didn't have to pay any money to get trained because I was already a teacher who had a master's degree. I didn't have to pay for rent because I worked out of my house. I didn't have to pay for marketing because I found ways to level the playing field and market for free. I didn't have to invest in expensive systems because I created my own. I never have to pay for architectural design changes because I can use a computer anywhere in my house. I had the computer. Later on, when I do plan to make changes to my office, it can all be tax deductible. Pretty sweet, right?

That isn't to say that I don't have any costs associated with running my business. Since I got started, I have found some tools to make my life a whole lot easier. They are worth the investment. I pay $300 a year for subscriptions to websites that are effective and engaging for students. I love using Stripe, my credit card processing company, which makes it easy to get paid. I set each client on an automatic payment plan. As of 2021, this currently costs 2.9% and +.30 for each transaction. I consider these costs "my assistants". No need to hire assistants, because Stripe collects payments with little effort from me.

I am able to deduct my own professional development on my taxes. I am a lifelong learner so that's good news for me. I've found it essential to invest anywhere between $1,000 to $4,000 each year, depending on my needs. You may not see this as necessary, but I know that I can always find the next piece of information that will take my business to the next level. Because my other expenses are low, it makes it easier to justify spending on the most helpful tools and training.

I highly recommend getting a business coach if you have never been in business before. I'm glad I did. I first began thinking about this need to have a business coach while I was watching the Olympics with my daughters. I noticed that every single Olympian had a coach. Not one person was doing it on their own. Then it dawned on me. All successful athletes have coaches; could I make my business more successful by having a coach? I got one and proved that yes, having a business coach could help my business be more successful. Remember, I was coming from the teaching world essentially and had 5 failed businesses. I didn't know what I was doing, so investing in a coach was essential to my success. A coach is able to take a look at where you are and guide you to where you need to be. A coach can also be your go-to person when you have business questions.

That is why I started The Online Tutor Coach, LLC. One of the biggest problems I had with working with coaches outside of the tutoring world was that they didn't understand the industry. At the Online Tutor Coach, every coach is a tutor who helps other tutors on the side. To work directly with a coach, go to www.onlinetutorcoach.com and click on store. If you scroll to the bottom, you will see several coaches you can work with to help meet the needs of your business.

Another strategy I used to grow my business savvy was joining mastermind forums. These were entrepreneur peer groups where we brainstormed answers to business questions that came up for us. This was the most beneficial investment that I made. My network now has so many people at my disposal that if I have a question, I can go directly to them without spending hours scouring the internet. Having that kind of support is amazing. It motivated me to develop the same type of support in the Jumpstart Program and my Insider Secrets Club for Online Tutors.

Figure 8.2 shows each of the costs that I incurred while growing my own business. The total cost for me in 2012 to have an ongoing tutoring company was $5,180. If I didn't set aside any money for professional development, it could cost me just $1,180 a year to run it. If you didn't have a business coach it would only be $680 and if you wanted, you could even get those costs down and get started just like I did with $0. Not bad. But I do choose to spend on these things because these expenditures help me beyond measure. Plus, I am able to subtract business expenses from my total income earned. Seeing that reduction in my taxes owed is a great benefit.

Resources	low	high
Membership websites	$0	$300
PayPal	$0	$300
Office supplies	$0	$50
Business cards	$0	$30
Business coach	$0	$500
Personal development	$0	$4,000
Total	**$0**	**$5,180**

Figure 8.2

Now that we have taken a look at what it takes financially to run an online tutoring business, let's take a look at what you can write off as a business expense. It is best practice to hire someone the first year to do your taxes who is familiar with small businesses. But until that time, you can save receipts and create an expense report to give to the person who will do your taxes.

The first thing you will want to do is create a file in your filing cabinet or file box. Name it, "Business Taxes 20_ _." Every time you purchase something that is listed below, you will have a place to put your receipt. Inside of your wallet or purse, designate a place to put receipts until you return home. This system saves you from searching through an endless pile of receipts later on.

As a business owner, you are allowed to write off business expenses that classroom teachers are cannot write off. You can track your expenses using an Excel spreadsheet and add to it each month so that when tax time comes, it is effortless.

I love to take trips, so I use the acronym TRIPS to help me with what I am allowed to write off as a business expense.

T = Travel
R = Running my business
I = Incurred costs
P = Personal Development
S = Supplies

TRAVEL

The first area that you will be able to take tax write-offs includes all of the travel expenses that relate to your business. You will be able to write off airfare, cabs, and food. All you need to do is hold onto your receipts and put them into your receipts folder for the current year. Update yourself on the current tax policies if you hope to combine business travel with personal travel; there are restrictions.

Taxpayers in the U.S. add up the receipts for airfare as one expense, cabs or travel as another expense, and all of your food as another expense. Then put the information in an Excel spreadsheet that is similar to the one listed in table 9.1.

It is important to note that everything is a 100% tax deduction except for food. Food is a 50% deduction because you would normally need to eat anyway, but typically eating out is more expensive when you are travelling.

RUNNING YOUR BUSINESS

Anything that you need to run your business can be written off. Here is a list of items that I am able to write off.

Membership sites
PayPal or Stripe fees
Computer
Internet
Phone
Marketing

As an online reading tutor, I utilize **www.raz-kids.com**, a site that gives me leveled reading. This goes on my expense report, and I write it off. The other membership sites that I am a part of I can easily write off as well.

You can also write off the expenses for a PayPal and Stripe processing fees. PayPal has slightly higher processing fees than Stripe and each has a per transaction fee. Be sure to keep track of these fees each month. Many tutors to pay extra taxes because they do not record everything. You will pay taxes as the employee and the employer, so you are already paying more tax. Take all of the deductions you can so that you will owe the least amount.

You need computer equipment. If you add equipment or if your computer equipment needs repair, you are able to write these expenses off. These items include headsets, mouse, actual computer, hard drive, and anything else needed for you to use your computer to run your business.

Another item that you can write-off is the amount of internet that you use for your business. For example, if you use 75% of the internet to run your business, then you can take the total amount spent on the internet each month and multiply that by 75% (x .75). That is the amount that can be deducted.

The same is true about the phone. If you have a separate line for your office then you can write that off. Most people run their business using their cell phone. If you used your cell phone 50% of the time for business and 50% of the time for pleasure, then you can deduct 50% of your phone bill.

Every penny that you spend on marketing is a tax deduction. Marketing supplies include flyers, paid advertising and so on. Canva, the user-friendly graphic design site, makes editing my marketing pieces something you can do yourself.

IN THE HOME

A percentage of your house can even be tax deductible. If this is something that you wish to do, you definitely want to talk to the person doing your taxes and decide if this is a good decision for you. Guidelines are strict.

If you have a certain sized home and use square footage to determine that 10% of that home is taken up by your office, then you can deduct that percentage of your mortgage payment. You can even deduct 10% of electricity since you need that to run your business. If you think about it, if you had a brick-and-mortar business, then you would have to pay these expenses. The government does not treat a brick-and-mortar small business much different than a home business.

Staying on top of house cleaning while running a business can be hard. Some people hire a cleaning company to come in and help. The proportion of the bill dedicated to office cleaning is another business expense to deduct. Use the office percentage to calculate this amount.

Not everything in your home is tax deductible and each state has its own laws. If you are in another country you will have to check with the laws of your country. This is why I highly suggest getting a tax accountant the first year to make sure that you are taking advantage of every benefit that you possibly can.

PROFESSIONAL DEVELOPMENT

There's always more information to learn. Whether you are learning more about owning your own business or getting professional development in the specific area that you are teaching online, you can deduct it. Here are some examples.

Conferences
Books
Professional organizations

Professional magazines
Professional membership sites
Networking groups
Jumpstart Your Online Tutoring Business Masterclass
Insider Secrets Group for Online Tutors

Any conferences that you attend can be a deduction. I usually attend the Wisconsin State Reading Association conference, International Literacy Association Conference, Homeschooling conferences, and Marketing conferences. All of these can be written off as a business expense.

Often when I hear about a book that contains the information that I need to grow my business or do something better, I go on Amazon and purchase it. Not only is it cheaper on Amazon, it is convenient. You can simply print a copy of your receipt, mark it in your expense report and put it in a file where you save a hard copy of all of your receipts.

I am a member of the International Literacy Association. My membership to the organization a write-off, and so is the monthly magazine that keeps me on top of best practices. What organizations might support your tutoring practice?

SUPPLIES

Lastly, you can write off any supplies that you need to run your business. Here is a list of some of the supplies that I use.

1. Notebooks
2. Binders
3. Staples
4. Paperclips
5. Tape

6. File folders
7. Pens/Pencils
8. Pencil Sharpener
9. Copier Paper
10. Printer ink or cartridges

Pretty much any office supply that you need can be a deduction. Some of these may seem like tiny things to worry about, but some of them are more expensive like printer ink. It all adds up, so it doesn't hurt to jot them down.

Table 9:1 shows what an excel spreadsheet that is used as an expense report could look like.

CONCLUSION

It is estimated that seventy percent of legitimate tax deductions could be deducted a home-based business can deduct completely go unclaimed each year. Don't add to that 70%. Take all the advantages that you can. You will be required to pay your own health insurance and save your own money for retirement, so these deductions can help you do that.

Expenses	Jan.	Feb.	Mar.	April	May	June	Year Total
Travel							
airfare							
transportation							
food							
Running your business							
membership sites							
PayPal/Stripe							
computer							
internet							
phone							
marketing							
In the Home							
electricity %							
mortage %							
Professional Development							
conferences							
books							
professional organizations							
professional magazines							
professional sites							
networking							
Supplies							
office supplies							
copy paper							
printer ink							
Total							

Table 9.1 Expense Report for running your business

Before I started the Jumpstart Program I struggled with putting myself out there and often second guessed myself. I felt like everything had to be perfect before putting any content out. Then nothing was getting done.

Then during the Jumpstart Program I was able to gain some momentum with posting things about my business, sharing my website, and putting myself out there. Having the accountability and support of the class helped me tremendously. It gave me the push I knew I needed to take with my business and I was able to book an additional 17 hours for myself!

Thank you Joanne for the continued professional development. I highly recommend tutors join the Jumpstart Masterclass because it gives you great networking opportunities with other tutors, confidence to grow your business, and support needed to keep pushing yourself each and every day!

Janay Wilkinsin

Online Reading Tutor

Step 2

ORGANIZED SYSTEMS

Organized systems need to be in place for your business to operate easily and efficiently. This section will give you a look at what you need to gather to do your tutoring and structure your business operation. You will begin to learn about creating a business plan and lifesaving online tools.

6 Figuring out your Niche and your Ideal Client for your Business Plan

Every successful company needs to start with a business plan when it comes to organization. In my Jumpstart[21] course. I walk people step by step into creating a successful business plan so they can figure out their mission, vision, and specific goals.

This chapter focuses on a critical part of your business plan. I will guide you as you think about the services you want to provide and how you will market them.

My first advice to any online tutor is to shift from being a generalist to tutoring a narrower subject and client base. The old adage, "Jack of all trades and master of none," is how potential clients are likely to view a tutor who says they teach a wide array of subjects. Choosing your niche will change this perception. A niche is an area in which you would consider yourself an expert. Your niche might be one of these: math, reading, or SAT preparation. Or a niche could be closely related courses, like geometry, trigonometry, and calculus.

An ideal client is a person you tailor your business to reach. You will need to get clear about what subject you want to tutor and who you want to teach. The clearer you can get, the more proficient you will become and the better your advertising outreach will be.

Some people want to teach everything to everyone. I tell people to keep their guard up for people like this because people who think they are great at everything are usually not very good. On the other hand, an expert is in demand and can afford to turn away business outside their expertise. You have the whole world at your disposal, so you don't have to worry about a shortage of clients for you.

Answer the following questions to get clear about your business.

1. What do you want to teach online?

    _____
    _____
    _____

2. Why should people come to you to teach it to them?

    _____
    _____
    _____

3. Who else is already good at what you want to do online?

    _____
    _____
    _____

4. What is the age range of your students?

    _____
    _____
    _____

5. Who is your ideal client?

_____

_____

_____

_____

_____

_____

_____

_____

_____

_____

_____

_____

_____

_____

_____

_____

_____

_____

_____

_____

You may have noticed that I have given you lots of space to figure out who your ideal client is. Do your best to describe this person. If you understand this client, you can target your advertising to find them. You can then speak to them in a specific manner, so people feel like you are talking to them personally. You will be more apt to attract your ideal client if you do this exercise.

When I first figured out who my ideal client would be, it looked like this.

Marissa is 34 years old, and she has graduated from college. She is going back to school for her MBA while working full-time at Kohl's corporate and taking care of her two kids, Melissa and Joey. Marissa desperately wants school to be easy for her kids and not have to struggle as she did. She wants the best for them and their education. Marissa is married, but her husband travels a lot. Many responsibilities for the home and the children fall on her. She wishes she could have more quality time with her kids, but with soccer practice, swim, school, and taking care of the house, there just isn't a lot of time.

Marissa sits down with Melissa every night to do homework, but Melissa resists her help. She frequently tells her mom that she is wrong and that she wishes dad was home to help her. This frustrates Marissa. Marissa doesn't understand why reading is so hard for her child. Even though she struggled through school, reading just seemed to come easy for her. She is lost in how to help her daughter and is looking for resources that she can tap into.

Marissa hates her job, which is why she is going back to school, but she knows she has to keep her job to help support her family. She is willing to do everything for her family, even stay in a position that she does not like. Her work and Melissa's struggles with school keep her up at night. When she is frustrated, she comes to blogs like mine, looking for tips and tricks that she can use with her daughter to make reading fun and not a chore.

Marissa values education and is willing to go to any lengths to ensure that her kids have a good education. When the kids go to bed, Marissa looks for ideas that she can implement in hopes of raising lifelong readers.

You may have noticed that I have given my ideal client a name. The people that you hope to attract are real people who have a set of real problems. What are those problems? What is your ideal client looking for from you? Why would your ideal client benefit from your services? Remember that you are in this business to be of service. You will market your services to a specific group of people. The more targeted you get, the more opportunity they have to find you. Even people that you are not targeting will find you. Then you are left with the tough decision of whether you will choose to work with them or not.

When I create my videos, I create them for this client. When I post messages on Facebook, I picture Marissa and speak right to her. When I create flyers, I keep her in mind to help her find me. I give specific advice to her on my blog and tweet tips to her during the day. I owe it to Marissa to make myself visible. She is looking for the services I provide, and I feel a duty to offer her a solution. My laziness could result in her child suffering even more.

Notice how I only focus on reading and how my ideal client is looking specifically for help with her daughter's reading. This clarity allows me to focus on one area and learn to stand out as one of the best. When you are one of many choices, can you afford to skip this step? Absolutely not.

If you have left the ideal client space blank, go back and fill it out. This is a critical step in your advertising and attracting the people you want to help. Skipping this step is not an option for those who seek success.

7 Favorite Online Organizational tools you can't live without

Technology is a pivotal part of my business. Without it, I'd have no way to support so many students and tutors. Some of the tools are cheap, and some of them are free, but these are tools that I use to run my business that I could not live without.

PASSWORD MANAGERS

Have you ever been frustrated at the number of passwords you must remember? If you use the same one over and over, you'll risk identity theft or worse. So, how can you keep track of hundreds of passwords? The answer is a password manager. Password managers supply a secure vault for your usernames and passwords. The best ones have a zero-knowledge policy so that your data is always encrypted and cannot be read or shared by them.

I use LastPass[22]. With **LastPass**, I only have to remember one password. LastPass is a digital vault and form filler that keeps track of usernames and passwords, so it automatically logs you into websites that require logons. I can access LastPass on any computer, so I don't need to keep a list of passwords or try a billion combinations to get into various websites. The only password I ever need is my LastPass password. I use the free version. Decide whether a free version is best for you or if you would benefit by being able to work across a spectrum of mobile and desktop devices for a small fee.

Password managers travel with you, letting you use multiple devices at home or while traveling. They will remember the sites you use, allowing you to reach them with a click, or a search. This feature is handy if you use other computers on a trip.

ZOOM

Zoom has given me financial freedom. I know that most people are familiar with it now, but when I got started, people either had not heard about it or were scared of it. I found this quite funny, but this was a real fear for people. As soon as I invited people onto a free assessment with Zoom, the online interaction convinced them that this would be a great platform to use. Your consultation can be an opening to prove that one-on-one sessions are highly engaging.

You may encounter people who fear Zoom due to security concerns and overuse during the pandemic. Since the pandemic, Zoom has tightened up its security so that random people can't hack into the system. You now can have people sign in with the link and a password or manually let people into your room so that only the people you want in the room are present.

With Zoom, you can share your screen with your students

and even have them write or annotate on your screen. If you want to share a video, just select 'share sound' when you share your screen, so your student will be able to hear the sound of the video. I love using videos from YouTube that teach simple concepts like two vowel talker or silent e.

You can also give yourself a professional background with the green screen feature. Some people find the stock blue background or the blur background feature to be less distracting. I like to insert a nice living room. Make sure you have good lighting, and it will look like you are there.

KOALA

Koala is a virtual meeting space that lets you create a fanciful online classroom. This 3D virtual classroom is a cross between Minecraft and Zoom. Your students roam around the room with you as avatars. I set up instruction boards ahead of time and keep adding to specific students' boards. You can save boards as templates and reuse them for future purposes.

The program keeps developing. Koala continues to listen to its users to add features requested by tutors and teachers. Watch a demo on my YouTube Channel: https://youtu.be/PzQBK-44Nf0 (While you visit, subscribe to my channel so that you can continue to get access to great content in the online tutoring world.)

ONE DRIVE AND GOOGLE DRIVE

One Drive and Google Drive store your files in the cloud rather than on your computer hard drive. With the discovery of One Drive, I can access resources from anywhere in the world. If you already have a Microsoft 365 license, you already have access to One Drive at no additional cost.

Now I can access everything effortlessly from various devices. It truly is fantastic. I also use Google Drive. You can check both of these out and see which one will be a better fit for you. Either may offer you a certain amount of free data storage.

Google Drive is a great resource to share files with someone else. When I share a link with the person, they can view it within their Google Drive. The beauty of file sharing this way is that you can both work on the file, and there are no worries about it being too large to be sent or impossible to download by the recipient. Many tutors have their students send their assignments to them ahead of the session so they can analyze it together. Sharing the file on Google Drive can be an excellent option.

PayPal or Stripe

At one point I probably would have objected to paying a transaction fee or a small percentage of a payment to a financial service. That is, until a client neglected their invoice or refused to pay me. PayPal and Stripe have become common payment options that steer clear of these problems. It has allowed me to take payments, send out invoices, and create automatic payments efficiently. Because of PayPal and Stripe, I only need to focus on billing and finances for 10 minutes a week. That means that I can run my business without paying someone to take care of this part.

PayPal and Stripe are safe places for people to pay you without worrying about the transaction. Their teams of anti-fraud experts protect you as the seller and your client as the consumer. PayPal and Stripe use secure servers and data encryption.

Also, PayPal stores all of the information about payments you have received. It is easy to access that information whenever you need it. I use it when I track my earnings each month. Also, I print a report to double-check when I do my taxes. PayPal takes care of all the calculations so that I do not have to.

PayPal charges a fee for each transaction and takes a percentage, just like a credit card company would do. As of 2021, each transaction costs .49 and PayPal takes 3.49% of the total paid to you.

Stripe is a little bit cheaper. They charge .30 per transaction and take 2.9% for the credit card transaction.

PayPal and Stripe also make it possible for you to sell internationally and teach clients abroad. This cuts out the hassle for you. When my Australian clients pay me, neither of us needs to calculate exchange rates. Just make sure that they choose USD if you are in the United States. The rest is all handled by PayPal.

YOUTUBE

YouTube has provided my business with an online presence of over 6,000 subscribers. It also gets found in Google on page 1 without me spending any money, and 53x quicker than it would without my YouTube presence. Wow, those are staggering statistics, just for storing my videos there.

I had created a video one time but hadn't done my keyword work yet. I was just going to get it published then figure out keywords later. I began to research my keywords and found one keyword that was sure to get excellent results. I edited the video title with the keyword, and within five minutes, I was on page one for that keyword. People spend a ton of money to get these results, and I was able to get them immediately because of YouTube. Now that is power.

YouTube is what I would consider the 500-pound gorilla for video marketing. It is the second biggest search engine in the world. So, if you want to get found to tutor kids or adults online, you need to be on YouTube. You are throwing thousands of dollars in potential income away if you don't.

So, I already know what some of my readers are thinking; that there is no way I will get on a camera. No worries, you don't have to. Another option is to stay off-camera but use your voice with text onscreen. You can prepare a series of images or slides to convey your content. A popular alternative is VideoScribe, a doodle illustration generator. You can create a ton of videos for free using VideoScribe. First, go to www.sparkol.com to access it. This program allows you to try it free for 7 days. During that time, you can create tons of videos to have at your disposal for YouTube or wherever you decide to use them. While you are at it, you might explore using VideoScribe for Educators, for instruction use with students.

Some of you may feel that you are not tech-savvy, so you might think this is outside your comfort zone. The Jumpstart Your Online Tutoring Business Masterclass has helped many tutors expand their reach using technologies like these. Jumpstart participants get videos, examples, coaching, and tech help to guide the way, step by step.

TUTORBIRD

TutorBird is an all-in-one platform for organizing your tutoring business. It supports tutor records, appointment calendars, attendance, and billing. TutorBird is an incredible tool for a tutor just getting started and indispensable for the fully-booked tutor.

You can get a 3-month trial for this program by using my special link for my community. Just go to **Facebook and Join the Ultimate Support Group for Online Tutors**. After you join the group, you can redeem this 3-month trial. **Sign Up for TutorBird Today! | TutorBird**[23]

With TutorBird, you will gather and store information about every student, including their credit card information. You can add your students to the calendar or give them a link to choose openings. TutorBird tracks each session used and accurately bills your working hours. Invoicing is automated. If you've stored their credit card info, you get paid immediately. You'll be free to focus on the most essential part of your business, your students.

If you decide to grow your business, Tutorbird supports you all the way. When you add additional tutors, there is one dashboard to access everything. Add other tutors' hours to the schedule and see yours as well. The app will calculate how much to pay each tutor each month, making your job easier.

There is a place for you to keep track of your taxes so that you can print off a report at the end of the year and just insert the information into TurboTax or give it to your accountant. This makes staying on top of your business easy.

In addition to all of these cool features, your students and parents have a portal they can access as well. If they need to reschedule a session within the parameters you set up, they can do that by logging in. No longer do the parents have to email you for reschedules. Also, you won't make errors on what time to do the makeup session.

This incredible service streamlines the business side of my business. The best part is that it is affordable for independent freelance tutors. At just $12.95 per month, it is worth every penny. I think you will love it.

COMMUNITIES

The online communities that I am a part of have always been lifesavers. Whenever I have a question about something, I know where I can go. I don't need to spend endless hours of research trying to figure something out. I can put my question out to the community, walk away for a couple of hours, and have several answers by the time I come back. That is time management at its best.

Some groups are free, like those found on LinkedIn and Facebook. Some communities require a paid membership or subscription.

I personally have a community that I have been building online that specifically helps people just getting started with their company. It's called It's called The Ultimate Support Group for Online Tutors[24]. This group is located on Facebook, where it's a closed group. The beauty of the closed group environment is that it stays separate from your regular Facebook page. You can ask questions or share answers without fear of it being seen by your clients or students. We share answers to questions and support and encourage each other every step of the way. All you need to do is request membership, and I will set up your access to the group.

When I started tutoring online, I felt like I had to do everything the hard way. I didn't know anyone I could contact for help like I could when I was in the school system. I tried to find people like me that were doing what I was doing and made some contacts, but they weren't quality contacts. I tried asking questions and being as helpful as I could in return, but it was hard. I had to learn everything by trial and error. I want to save you time and money so that it doesn't take you three years to finally have the systems in place that will make your job easy.

I live by the philosophy that we are all in this together and can support each other in incredible ways. I don't tutor everything to everyone, so I like to suggest another great tutor in the online world that can support my clients. I do this free of charge because people do this for me on a regular basis. What would a community of people like that mean to you? For me, it is priceless.

The community is also a place to share things that maybe aren't working and get suggestions from people who have been doing the things you have been doing. Each week there are live streams and free pieces of training available to support you on your path to greatness.

When tutors were asked what their experience has been like in the Ultimate Support Group for Online Tutors they said,

 Dori Osmond
I wouldn't be where I am today without this group.

Like · Reply · 1d

 Anna Maria D'Ippolito
Feeling supported and glad to have opportunities to support others.

Like · Reply · 1d

 Daniela Lochan
This group has been a wonderful blessing to my business. The support, and all the information shared here are fantastic!! Thank you!!

Like · Reply · 1d

Step 3

MARKETING

8 Where Will I Get My Students?

Are you wondering where you will ever get enough clients to make the income that you desire? Do not worry, remember to keep your focus on the things that you do want and they will come easily for you. This chapter is going to begin to touch on some of the marketing tools to make sure you always have the number of students that you desire.

Since 2012 I have been teaching different marketing techniques to tutors. As new online tools emerge to get students, I stay on top of it so that you have the ability to take advantage of everything at your fingertips. Let's start with the basics.

First, you want to let everyone know what you are currently doing now as an online tutor. When I began fifty percent of my clients were people that I knew or had met personally. The other 50% come from the internet and referrals.

Today it is 100% from the internet and referrals. The best part is I don't have to let people know what I am doing anymore. People seek me out and this can happen for you as well.

REFERRALS

When I was selling Usbourne books I had a tough time getting people to book a party. I had to offer lots of free stuff in order to entice them to book and event and invite their friends. If you have ever been involved in a direct sales company like this then you know what I am talking about.

Your tutoring business is going to be nothing like that. People love giving referrals of excellent services. They love referring great people. Sometimes you won't even have to ask them to do it. You'll ask someone for a testimonial, and you will learn that they have already been telling friends about you and your tutoring.

When someone refers a client to me, the client never feels that their friend only refers them to get something out of it. They are referring the service because they are genuinely with their child's educational success. They want their friends and family to feel that thrill, too.

Everyone leaves that conversation feeling like a winner. The person who referred feels happy because they know they are passing on a great name and a great service to their friend. The person getting the referral feels like they are in great hands before they start working with the tutor.

At one time, another parent referred my services because she knew what I did. She had three girls in the same classes as my girls. She wasn't sure if I was good at what I did, but she knew that I did reading tutoring online.   She gave her friend my website and passed the information along. The woman contacted me. I gave her daughter a free assessment, report, and a free first session. Before the free trial was over, she mentioned that she had already started to see results.

After three months of tutoring her daughter in reading, the girl went from being at the bottom of her class at the end of first grade to the top of her class beginning second grade. Her daughter increased her reading level 3 full grades with just 12 hours of instruction.

This parent was obviously very happy about those results. When she caught up to her friend, she said, "Wow, you know great people."

See how this was a win-win for everyone? I did nothing except make sure that people knew what I did. I didn't do it in a way that was obnoxious or annoying. I simply had conversations with her about what I did when she asked. It was natural and not salesy in any way.

SKIP BUSINESS CARDS AND DO THIS INSTEAD

Everyone thinks that you should use business cards when you are networking. I did in the beginning. First, I created a cute name for my business, which was Bright Idea Reading Tutoring. Then I made business cards with a website that was free instead of buying a domain name. As soon as I paid for a domain name, all of my business cards were obsolete and I had to purchase new ones.

Today, I have found a better strategy than business cards. While business cards can be useful if you are doing networking events or attending conferences, most tutors do not engage in this kind of networking. Typically, you will be out and about when you chat with people about what you do.

Perhaps you are volunteering at church, exercising in class, or picking up a cup of coffee at your local Starbucks. There are opportunities around every corner.

At church I had a member mention to me how their child was struggling with reading. Most people knew what I did. Some people might awkwardly give a business card at this point. That will not close the sale. I can guarantee it.

Instead ask more about what the child is struggling with. Find out what the parent is noticing and what the teachers at school are saying. Next, invite the parent to a free assessment with their child on Zoom. If they say yes, then ask for their best email that you can use to send them the details later. This way, you are in the driver's seat the entire time.

If you just give them your business card, then the parent forgets, loses the card, or doesn't take the next step. The more you can guide them in taking the next step, the more likely they will do as you say versus staying on the fence or searching for a different tutor.

In fact, 100% of the people that I have used this process with have moved forward to become a client. Give it a try and see if it can be effective for you. I guarantee more people will follow you step by step through the process and they don't feel weird or hassled because you are following up. These people want you to follow up.

This is a part of being professional. Many tutors think that they are bothering the person who showed interest, but they are more annoyed when you don't follow through than when you do. This is not harassing them. Harassing them would be to continue to call them when they asked you not to. Following through is just professional. Be a professional freelance tutor. People will respect you more and refer you to their friends and family.

SIBLINGS

Families often ask me to work with more than one of their children. I have worked with brothers, sisters, twins, cousins, and so forth. I have even had people ask me to shift from one of their kids who had improved to begin working with another child.

You will really know your service is worthwhile when parents keep coming up with other ways to use your services. They don't want to give you up.

I never advertise that I work with kids in math, but I will for students, past students, or siblings. I focus on teaching the essential reading skills needed to succeed with math. I have found that if a child struggles with reading and is struggling in math, it is usually because of word problems and math vocabulary. Those are my two favorite areas to tackle.

E-MAIL SIGNATURE

A resource I use to make my email look professional is called WiseStamp[25]. WiseStamp not only signs my email automatically, but it also promotes me. My email signature has a picture of me, the title of my company, "The Online Reading Tutor," my website, and ways to find me on Facebook and YouTube. It rotates through testimonials and links to helpful content.

Anyone who clicks on those tabs will see my social media presence, and anyone that I send an email to can find me and see what I do. It is amazing how having this one tool gives me free promotion of my services.

In one instance, WiseStamp opened a whole new avenue for potential clients. The president of the PTO solicited silent auction baskets to raise money for my daughters' school library. I replied by email that I could put together a basket and get back to her by the end of the day. Seeing my signature, she asked if I did tutoring for reading. I explained my business very briefly. She said, "Why don't you make a basket that revolves around your company?" She put business cards by the basket for potential customers at the auction, getting the word out on my tutoring.

Wow, this was all because of using WiseStamp and having my information on my email signature. I honestly don't think I would have used this opportunity to promote myself. I just like to be of service. So, I got my name out there to a high-end clientele for free. I didn't have to put any effort into it besides gathering a basket. I included a free coupon for services, some autographed books I wrote and some school supplies in the basket.

LinkedIn

If you are not on LinkedIn yet, then get on LinkedIn. This professional social media site will help you establish and grow your credibility. Begin by filling your profile with your experience working as a teacher or tutor.

Once you've set up your LinkedIn profile, gradually search out your contacts a few at a time, and invite them to connect with you. Include past and present colleagues and your contacts from other circles. I would love to connect with you on LinkedIn. Just type in Joanne Kaminski, and you will find me.

The "Endorsements" feature lets others acknowledge your talents in your field. I received an email from LinkedIn saying that I am in the top 1% of most recommended people for tutoring because of people's endorsements. The best part is, I didn't do anything to get that. I just listed the areas that are my expertise; my connections began endorsing me. I didn't even ask them to do that. LinkedIn sent them all the information and gave them the tools to endorse me. The secret to LinkedIn is to make sure you fill out your profile information at 100%.

Also, I ask my clients to write a recommendation on my LinkedIn page if they have liked the work I have done. People know that testimonials on a website could be fake, but you can't fake a great recommendation on LinkedIn. If you have recommendation after recommendation on this site, people will automatically see you as an expert in your field.

WEBSITE

If you are wondering whether you need a website as a professional freelance tutor, the answer is yes. Just go to Wix.com, for a site builder tool that is drag-and-drop simple. Thank goodness, creating a website has become much easier.

In the past, WordPress was dominant in this space, but some of us need a little more support. If you add a plug-in to your website, you can break your website and have to pay someone to get it back up. I like the support I find at Wix[26]. Everyone I chat to about this topic tells me they wish they had found me earlier and listened to my advice. Just go with something simple like Wix.com.

With Wix, you can create as many pages as you like. On your first page, include a welcome video that speaks to your ideal student. Video has a huge impact on how people will connect with you. Right away, you can personally thank them for visiting your website and connect with them even though you are not personally there in live time to greet them.

In addition, you will want to include an "about me" page. Think about telling your story from the perspective of the student. Did you ever struggle in the area that your students struggle in? Were you the person that was always helping other kids in your class? Tell your story from that perspective versus what school you went to, how many years you taught, or why you love teaching.

Also, think about sharing the types of results that you get with your students. Are you able to take students getting C's and D's to A's and B's? Can you increase the SAT score by 200 points? Take a look at your past students and discover the measurable results you can help new students achieve.

Most tutors say that their students become more confident, but that is not a measurable result. Be specific on how they become more confident. For example, they feel less stress when taking tests or are no longer afraid to read out loud to the class.

Make sure to include a contact page. Sometimes people just want to fill this out and chat with you immediately about working with their child or ask questions before getting started.

One more thing you want to do throughout is adding a call to action. For this, you shift from informing to asking them to take the next step toward becoming a client. Think about what the next step is that you want people to take after they've discovered you at your website. Is it to book a free consultation or get a free assessment? Is it to get a free item by giving their email? Make sure this call to action is on each page. While you think they will come to your home page first, their search results could land them on any page of your website.

BLOG

On your website you can also include a blog. Google and other search engines will find you more easily if you have added current content versus maintaining a static website. Do you know how many websites are placed on the internet each day? Tons. Remember what I said before, people will not find you by accident, so you need to be strategic.

Blogging is a great way to get found for your expertise. Write about things you know. Blog posts that have tips for improvement in an area you tutor may be exactly what your ideal client is searching the web to find. If they were to find your blog with descriptions of the challenges their child faces and strategies that give them hope in your blog, contacting you may be their next step. Make sure to use keywords and key phrases to create content that will attract your ideal parents and students.

FACEBOOK

If you are already on Facebook, then it will be easy to just start telling people what you are doing with your tutoring business. You can post updates with how it is all going for you and how excited you are. Your friends will want to promote you, so let them.

You will want to create a business page on Facebook and invite all your friends and contacts to like you. This again will show credibility so that when others look you up you have social proof.

Recently, I was thinking about doing business with a guy who claims to be a specialist in a certain area. I went to his page expecting to see how he is a specialist in this area, but I noticed he had an extremely small crowd. Don't be like him. Get yourself out there on the internet. If you are running an online tutoring company, people want to see a social media presence that is strong, not weak. People will trust you more if you show that you have following and have built an online presence. If you have a small following people may put up their guard and decide not to trust you. The result can be a loss in business.

CRAIGSLIST

Some tutors put an ad on Craigslist for $5. As of this writing, a $5 ad runs for 30 days.

When you are filling out the Craigslist form, all you need to do is check the category *services offered* and then a new screen will come up and you will select *lessons and tutoring*. From here you will need to write up a description of your service.

I did an interview with Rom JB who owns a Tutoring Agency in New York. He uses Craigslist almost exclusively to get students. Check out his description of what to include in your ad. **https://youtu.be/5VK_AtIwH_8A**

Things to include to make your Craigslist ad pop are,
1. Emojis
2. Testimonials
3. Images
4. Description of what you tutor
5. Results your students get
6. Contact information

Follow Rom's tips and you will get more students from your Craigslist ad. He even sprinkles emojis across his title. It boosts him higher in the search output. Also, think about using words that your ideal client uses to describe their situation. Share what the problem is that they may be experiencing and how you can be the solution.

Not all countries use Craigslist. There are similar platforms like Kijiji in Canada and Gumtree in the UK, so search for them if you live outside the USA.

Beware that there are scammers on these sites too. As long as you go into it knowing what to look for, you will be safe. For example, if a person talks about you cashing a check and is not concerned at all with the child and what they are struggling to learn, do not trust them. It is a scam.

The easiest way to tell if someone is a scammer is by asking about their child and getting them to tell you more about what they are struggling to overcome. Scammers don't know how to answer this question and are terrible at making stuff up. They will refuse to set up a free consultation with you on

Zoom and will never have a child you can meet.

There are other tools like Thumbtack where you pay for leads that are interested in the specific tutoring that you offer. You pay for each lead that contacts you and you can decide how many people you want contacting you each month. Not everyone turns into a student, but it is a cheaper alternative to ads on Google or Facebook. (Word of caution- Do not create a Google or Facebook ad unless you have experience in the marketing world.) Tutors that do not have experience get sucked in with the false image that they will create an ad and get a student. What usually happens is Facebook and Google eat up your funds and you are left with zero students. Stay far, far away in the beginning until you have more experience.

YOUTUBE

My favorite type of advertising is to make videos. I personally like making videos and playing with my keywords because I can get found very easily this way. In fact, if you type in "online tutor business coach," you will find one of my videos on the first page. People these days seldom look past the first page. They figure that the best information is either on the 1st, 2nd, or 3rd page. If what the person is looking for is not on one of those pages, then they usually just try another search. First page ratings will be pivotal to your business.

You might think that you don't like being on camera. No worries. You can make videos easily without having to have your face on camera. I have made a ton of these. One program I have used is called Videoscribe[27]. This service has a free trial period of 7 days. From there it only costs $19.99 a month. If you wish, you can make all your videos in one month and cancel it if isn't a method you want to continue using.

Another way to make a video is to use Zoom. You can hit record and start talking. The video will upload to your computer and you can then edit it. You can also share your screen and create a tutorial video if you wish. Creating videos provides helpful content to people looking for you and make yourself stand out as an expert without having to put your face on the camera.

Today it is easy to edit your videos. I use WeVideo, but you can also use the software that comes on your computer. This would be iMovie or Windows Media Player. You can also use your iPhone or iPad.

Making videos can be that easy. If you combine one of your videos with a blog post then Google will reward you even more as long as you are entering the keywords properly. In the Jumpstart Program I teach people how to do SEO marketing and find the keywords that will put them on page 1 of Google and many other search engines. SEO stands for search engine optimization. SEO is what makes your website more findable. You start by thinking about what people are typing into the search bar and then create content that matches that so your ideal parent and student can find you.

9 Building Trust with Potential Online Clients

We owe it to our potential clients to show the most authentic side of ourselves online as we can. People have their guard up when they are online. They believe that there are two different worlds out there. There is the world we live in where we evaluate everyone's faults and weaknesses, and then there is the online world where people can present themselves as they are something that they are not.

At this point in time, anyone can be an online tutor. There are no restrictions, and this is a position that people <u>do not need</u> credentials for, unless they apply to a company.

Those of us that do have credentials want to use that to our advantage. You will set yourself up as an expert if people can go on LinkedIn and see what your experience has been with teaching, what your credentials are educationally, and look at your endorsements and recommendations.

Anyone who thinks all they need to do is put a website up to start their business and just tell people about their company is sadly mistaken. You need to begin to build a relationship with people online and interact with them, not just blow your horn for your own benefit.

A helpful book I recommend is Engagement from Scratch![28] It is written by some of the top creators of phenomenal communities of trust online. Dany Iny is a co-author and a co-founder of Firepole Marketing. If you want to interact with people in a meaningful manner online, then you have to get a copy of this book.

Have you found that people will friend you on Facebook and never introduce themselves to you? The questions that automatically comes to my mind are, "Why do they want to friend me? Do they want to spy on me? Do they want to just make it look like they have a lot of friends, or do they want to sell me something?"

This is not a great way to build up trust, is it? Seriously, people are not clear online and for whatever reason people feel more important if they have 1,000 friends on Facebook rather than 200. Some people friend only people that they know and try to lock up their Facebook world. I am pretty nice and will friend everyone who wants to be friends. If people are trying to sell me something and aren't interested in being what I would call a "friend," or they are constantly sending me marketing messages, then I just unfriend them.

I allow people to watch me online and find out as much as they can because I am secure in who I am and what people will see me doing online. I am not afraid to have an online presence because a large part of what I do is online. Remember that 100% of my clients find me online, so if they feel more comfortable sitting in the back row and watching me for a little while, I am okay with that.

I think that it is important to get to know the differences

between the social media platforms out there. Facebook and Twitter are places comparable to the grocery store and my kids' school events. I can be casual, laid back, and just share in the glory of life with them. LinkedIn is my professional presence. I consider this the present-day resume. I mostly only put information on there that is about my business, successes that I have had, or allow other people to put all of their endorsements and recommendations about me on there. I don't share information about my kid's soccer game; that is information that I share on Facebook.

Also, in LinkedIn there are interest groups you can join. I join parenting groups, online teaching groups, and groups that relate to my business here. You are allowed to join 40 groups. You can interact and engage with people and in each of these groups. When you join, think about adding value in every way you can. Give more than you take and it will pay off.

Another way to gain trust from your potential online clients is to always be prompt. If you give people a time to meet on Zoom, make sure to be there when you say you will be there. If your system takes a while to log in, allow that time. If you are late even a couple of times, you could lose a student.

The most important thing is to be authentic and be who you are in the real world. If you wouldn't say something to someone's face, then don't say it online. Also, no one is attracted to people that complain all of the time online or off. They don't like people who having contentious arguments back and forth with others in the community. Always put your professional side forward so that people can be genuinely attracted to you.

10 Testimonials

Testimonials seem to be everywhere. If you check out other successful businesses, you will find testimonials. They are of the most important marketing tools at your disposal. In this chapter we are going to delve into why you need testimonials, how to get testimonials, and where to put testimonials. You will learn the different versions of testimonials and be able to start collecting them and using them in ways that best support your business.

So, why do businesses need testimonials? Testimonials show outcomes. Today it is all about social proof and if you don't have social proof, then you will not attract enough students to meet your goals or replace your income.

Today, people search online for anything they want to know. If they can't find information about you online, they will be wary about the services that you provide. Testimonials allow those searching to see other people's experience with you.

In the old days, when a business wanted referrals, they would offer special deals to customers who would refer contacts to them. You had to give them 10 names, addresses, and e-mails in order to get a special deal. Most businesses no longer practice this. No one wants to be on the other end of that. What would you think of a friend that gave your information away to a business just to get something at a reduced rate? I call these people users. Thank goodness I don't have friends like this today.

Now take a look at the friend who has valued your services so much that they give you a testimonial. They tell all of their friends about you because of the difference you made in their life. Now, instead of ten people who are probably going to dislike the fact that you gave away their information, you are left with people who sincerely want to pass your business information along to others. Testimonials give people the opportunity to tell their friends and the rest of the world the benefits they have received because of working with you. People are touched by this emotionally and want to move forward in doing business with you. They can see that you have benefitted others and they are hoping that you can benefit them as well. Testimonials provide the avenue for your business to grow in a healthy way.

Also, I want you to take a look at testimonials from another viewpoint. Do you enjoy talking about yourself and all of your successes? If you live in the United States, we don't always look highly on people who do this. We call them braggarts. The amazing things that you could say about yourself and your services go unsaid because you may not want to be viewed that way, but a testimonial is different. Testimonials allow other people to say what you can accomplish in a way that is authentic. When other people say it, that is their experience. It can't be denied.

Unfortunately for me, I had to learn this the hard way. When I first found out that I could close the reading gap a full year with just 8-12 hours of instruction, I wanted to share that with everyone. But many people just didn't believe me. Then people started to see what my clients were saying. Side note, if the parents of one of my students is on LinkedIn, I also connect to them to leave their testimonial there.

Here is what one client, Mandy McCumber said.

Joanne Kaminski tutored our 7-year-old daughter in reading this summer. She achieves results that are nothing short of miraculous. In the course of three short months, my daughter's reading improved by 2 1/2 grade levels!

From the first session, we found Joanne to be warm, engaging, and fun. Her enthusiasm for teaching children to read is contagious, and my daughter looked forward to their sessions. Through her blog, Joanne engaged me in the learning process as well. She has some reading tricks that gave my daughter the tools to figure out words by herself, which I believe has set my daughter up for an amazing educational future. Meeting for tutoring sessions through Skype was gentle on the family schedule and very convenient. Her prices are reasonable, and my husband loved that she offered a discount for paying in lump sum.

I only wish we could clone Joanne so she could reach more children. She is gifted. I have no hesitations in recommending her to any parent of a struggling reader.

I only tutored her daughter 1 hour a week and we had these amazing results. Now my social proof has just sky rocketed because of this.

Here is what another client said.

Joanne is an outstanding tutor, with so many creative ways to engage children to improve their reading she's amazing. My son started online reading sessions with Joanne after we discussed his frustrations in reading. He was in 1st grade barely reading at a kindergarten grade level. This was causing social and self-esteem issues with him. He worked with Joanne about once a week during two school years. He finished his second grade at an actual second grade reader. Once he started working with Joanne he looked forward to the online sessions, because she made reading more fun for him! He clearly became a more confidant reader, and I could not have done it without the extra help from Joanne. I would recommend Joanne as a tutor to anyone who asked.

Then there is more. Here is what another client said.

Joanne has succeeded with my son where other educators have not. Her individual focus allows insight into the best learning style for my child and she has the ability to create a structure that keeps him motivated. His reading has improved tremendously as a direct result of her efforts. We are truly blessed and thankful to have Joanne and I wholeheartedly recommend her to any parent who has a son or daughter struggling with reading.

An adult client shared her story with me and I simply asked her if she would be willing to put a recommendation on LinkedIn. She said that she would love to and here it is.

Joanne was willing to step outside of her normal world and take on an adult student (myself). She works with me on the thing I need to work on and keeps us on track to use time well. I love that it is so easy to do by Skype! Joanne can be more than just a tutor, it's hard

to explain as an adult with Dyslexia she has become a sort of life coach and healer. She is very observant and will find the things that you need to help you how you want and need to be helped. Only good things have come from the time that Joanne has worked with me in this Skype Tutoring! Just as a person I can't say enough good things about her. Then add that she is the best at what she does for anyone with reading trouble! She will find a way to help! Working with Joanne continues to empower me, that I know I can do these things that I struggled with for so long. Thank you, Joanne for being you!
I Recommend Joanne to anyone looking for a reading tutor for any reason!!!!!

A loyal customer, Renee Love

I am so proud of the amount of progress that Renee has made. She started off thinking that she was reading at a fifth-grade level. Now she confidently reads high school and college level material.

I love that LinkedIn posts a person's picture along with their comment. When people read their testimonials in LinkedIn, it is inescapable that a real person has shared their experience with me as an online reading tutor.

Here is the thing to realize. The clients you help often don't know how to return the favor other than paying your fees. All you have to do is to point them in the right direction. Clients often write me an email giving me feedback, sharing how I have been helpful to their child. I thank them and ask if they would be willing to share a recommendation on LinkedIn. Once they say yes, I send them a request. Usually, within a week, the people happily write the recommendation.

These days, you will find that those testimonials happen in written form and in video. Not everyone is willing to capture a testimonial with you on video, but some will prefer to.

A video is even more potent in my mind than a written testimonial. Above, Renee shared her story about Skype tutoring in writing. Go to this link to see her video testimonial.
http://www.youtube.com/watch?v=E0V0BKIwars

The video is about 10 minutes long, but viewers will notice the emotion it creates.

Some of you may be thinking, "But I have never taught online before, so I don't have anyone that can give me a testimonial!" That doesn't mean that you can't sell your services without one. In fact, when I started tutoring, I had the President of the school where I last taught give a recommendation. Here is what she had to say.

I have never met anyone as enthusiastic about teaching children to read as Joanne! Her ability to engage children in ways that facilitate a love of reading is impressive. Joanne is organized and hard-working with a positive attitude. She is also innovative and always thinking of new and different ways to do the work that she loves. Joanne is a literacy expert!

If past clients are willing to leave a recommendation for you, repeat these testimonials on your website. People will be more apt to hire you. Potential clients checking your website and social media consider whether to invest their hard-earned dollars. They will be sold on someone who has clients vouching for them, thrilled with their results.

Write down the names of the people who you could ask for a testimonial that supports what you want to do as an online tutor. Next, contact them and see if they would be willing to help you out.

1. _____
2. _____
3. _____
4. _____
5. _____

Sometimes people don't give a testimonial because they don't know what to write. I have found that I can ease this fear by giving them some questions they can use create the perfect testimonial. Those questions are:

1. How did you find me?
2. What was your child struggling with before we started working together?
3. What results did your child get?
4. What was it like working with me?

Each of these questions is powerful. The first question deals with how people discovered you. When people read it, they can automatically connect with the person leaving the testimonial. For example, if a client said, "I found Joanne on Google," the person reading the testimonial might think, "Hey I found her on Google, too."

The second question is another connection point. Parents reading the testimonial of a parent whose child struggles with sounding out words might connect with that because their child is also struggling with sounding out words.

The next two questions bring people into the dream. When

people are seeking out a tutor it is because they have a problem. When others can see you as the solution to the problem, they get excited about working with you. Asking parents to write down in their own words the results they saw their child achieve becomes a dream for the reader of the testimonial. The reader thinks about how they would love for their child to get that result.

The last question shares what is like working with you. Some people will be mention how flexible, caring or professional you are. Others mention how you good you make them feel. These are the kind of people that others like to work with.

Don't be afraid to ask people to write a testimonial for you. People rarely do it without being asked. Even people you ask may not get back to you. That is ok, just keep doing the best job you can and keep asking. Over time you will get so many positive reviews people will be dying to work with you.

Step 4

SERVICES

11 Free Assessment and Free Report

One of the secret strategies that has worked for me when it comes to providing top-notch services is giving each of my clients a free assessment. Some of you might be thinking, "Why in the world would you give away a $200 service for free?" Well, the answer is simple; it doesn't cost me anything except for a little bit of time. It gives me a benchmark, and it helps to build rapport.

Other tutoring companies will assess a child for a fee and present a plan to the family. The family often decides they don't have that kind of money for the services. However, when I give away the assessment and then hold the sales conversation directly afterward, people want to move forward with tutoring.

Think about it like this. You go to a car dealership. They ask if you would like to give this car for a spin. What if you needed to pay $200 plus gas to take the test drive? What would your response to this salesperson be?

If you are like me, your response is, "No, thank you." So, you go to another dealership, and you say, "Look, I just want to test drive this car and see if it works." The salesman says, "Sure, here are the keys. I hope you like it." There is no hassle. Taking a test drive was easy; you like the car. You are likely to decide to put down the money and pay for it. The experience is positive.

We live in a society that likes to test things before buying them. Why? Because there is a lot of junk out there. We don't want to get stuck with junk, things that don't work, or services that disappoint us.

From the very moment that your potential clients make contact with you, you want to deliver the most personable experience that you can. You are being watched. People will buy services from people they feel like they know, like, and trust. So be that person that people can know, like, and trust.

When you give away the assessment, people begin to think of you as caring. We like to do business with caring people.

Here is a business philosophy that guides my assessment. Business philosophy #1 = Under promise and Over deliver.

I'll share with you the secret formula that I use for all of my assessment reports. Here it is.

> Introduction
> Assessment results: text and graphs explaining results
> Overall Observations
> Instructional plan

You can use this formula with almost any type of tutoring that you provide. Customize the sections that pertain to your assessment and the data you collect and analyze.

Introduction

The introduction is the place to relay the information you have received from the parent through phone conversations, e-mail, and the registration form. Start with the child and what has been revealed to you as the problem. From the beginning of the report, you acknowledge the problems as the parent understands them. This shows that you have been paying attention to their child's specific needs and helps explain why you have given the child the specific assessments you have chosen.

Here is an example of an introduction for a recent client.

Child A is a 5th grade student in Canada going into 6th grade in the fall. He has been struggling with reading since kindergarten and diagnosed with ADHD in second grade. He has also been diagnosed with a broad-based learning disability. His school has been utilizing the Barton Reading and Spelling program and his parents have been helping Child A with this at home. According to Parent A, Child A is on level 3.

Child A has had many different tutors that have tried to help him with his reading. Unfortunately, they have been unable to help Child A succeed. He has made minimal progress and as a direct result does not enjoy reading or having to read. He does not feel comfortable with reading out loud in class and only is asked to do so when he has a book report to do.

Child A has had an online reading tutor previously that was injured and unable to work in the school. She was a classroom teacher for 25 years and had tons of previous experiences that she lists on her website. After working with Child A for 4 days a week for a month the family was unable to see any drastic improvement and discontinued her services.

Child A has suffered with his reading for a long time and still has hopes and dreams to become a pilot. His dad does not see college being in Child A's future due to his difficulties with learning. However, both mom and dad want to see Child A succeed no matter what his future holds and believe that knowing how to read at a certain level is a priority.

Parent A has been told that Child A is reading at a 2nd grade level. He has noticed that Child A guesses a lot when he reads and that his decoding ability is very weak. Below are the observations about Child A and his current reading level.

From this introduction can you see that I have been paying attention to the needs of the child and the family. I address every piece of information that is relevant to this child and his instruction.

Results

Now, the easy part is going through the assessment and providing the results. I will give you an example of one of my assessments, but if you don't tutor in reading, think about what this part could look like for you. If possible, quantify the measurements.

Phonological Awareness

Child A was able to easily find rhyming words, identify rhyming words, and produce rhyming words.

Child A was also able to put two sounds and three sounds together to figure out a word but struggled when it came to 4 sounds and 5 sounds. This is a task that most 2nd graders are able to complete without any problems. Students who struggle with this task that are in the 5th grade usually have dyslexia.

Sight Words

Child A has a huge gap in his ability to read sight words. The program that he is receiving instruction from currently focuses highly on phonics and does not include strategies for figuring out sight words. This helps explain why he is at the kindergarten instructional level for sight words.

Child A's other learning disabilities and information from his dad suggest that Child A may have some long-term memory issues that make it difficult for him to remember words that he has learned from one session to the next. Joanne is going to keep a close eye on this to see how it may affect the sessions that she has designed for him.

	Independent	Instructional	Frustration
Pre-Primer		x	
Primer		x	
1st grade		x	
2nd grade			x

Sight Word Analysis

One thing that the assessor noticed about Child A's reading is that he was able to read the closed pattern words pretty well. He seemed to struggle with sight words, words that do not seem to fit any of the vowel patterns and multisyllabic words.

Child A tends to use the beginning and ends of the words to figure them out. About 96% of the time, he is using the beginning and 58% of the time he is using the end. The area that Child A struggles with the most is the middle. This is usually where the vowel is located or the vowel patterns determined.

This data is in correlation with the level that Child A is at with the Barton method. He has progressed through level 1 phonemic awareness and level 2 consonants and short vowels. He is currently on level 3 where the focus is closed patterns and units. He will do well with the method of teaching that Joanne uses because she continues to work with these patterns, but also work with sight words in a way that will help him progress with his reading.

Correct Word	Error	Beginning	Middle	End
what	wit	x		x
animal	amil	x		x
were	where	x		x
want	went	x		x
who	how			
write	worked	x		
place	please	x		x
bear	beer	x		x
find	fund	x		x
sound	sond	x		x
thought	thogunt	x		x
knew	know	x		x
afraid	after	x		
moving	mon	x		
tired	teered	x	x	x
pieces	passes	x		x
picked	pitchered	x		x
though	thug	x		
clue	culg	x		
breathes	birth	x		
insects	insent	x		
weather	wither	x		x
noticed	nots	x		
money	morning	x		
		96%	4%	58%

Words in Context

Child A read kindergarten words at an Independent level. Words in context at the first-grade level however were frustrational for him.

	Independent	Instructional	Frustration
Pre-primer	x		
Primer	x		
1st grade			x

Words in Context Error Analysis

While reading words in text Child A relied significantly on the beginning of the word. About 83% of the time, he had the correct beginning sound. When reading in context vs. isolation he relied less on the end of the word. He also identified that he did not know the word and didn't have a strategy for the word in some cases.

When the whole page was text, Child A seemed to be easily overwhelmed. He was quickly relieved when the assessor told him that she would not have him read another passage after the 1st grade passage.

Correct Word	Error	Beginning	Middle	End
me	my	x		
spring	summer	x		
then	they	x		
man	mad	x		
kitchen	chen		x	x
heard	had/hadn't/hold	x		
decided	didn't	x		
sell	see	x		
ad	an	x		
paper	pepper	x		x
many	main	x		
wanted	until			
visit	vit	x		x
came	can	x		
they	there	x		
heard	had	x		x
afraid	after	x		
try	tear	x		
house	family			
heard	hadn't	x		
we'll	we	x		
		83%	5%	17%

Comprehension 6-16-12

Child A's comprehension seemed to be heavily linked to how well he read the passage. If he read most of the words correctly, then he was able to answer the questions without a problem. The more errors he had, the less he was able to understand what he was reading.

	Independent	Instructional	Frustration
Pre-Primer	x		
Primer	x		
1st			x

So that is the actual assessment from one of my students. I know everything that this child is able to do and everything that he needs to know to become a better reader. I have also noticed that the child most likely has dyslexia, which is why he is struggling so much and slowly have started sharing this information through the report.

Overall Observations

The overall observations section is a place where you can take the information from the introduction and the information from the assessment to give an overall view of what this child is able to do up to this point. State what the actual reading level is so that the parent doesn't have to guess. Tell parents that if the report is too confusing, all they have to do is look at the introduction, overall observations, and the instructional plan. If the parent needs to know more, then they can certainly look through each of the results, but it is not necessary.

Here is an overall observation regarding the same child. This is to give a complete picture for you.

The assessor has noticed that Child A may have dyslexia. An additional diagnosis from a psychologist would only be suggested if it would help to get the services that Child A would need from school staff to support Child A. Otherwise, there would not be a benefit for getting the diagnosis.

Child A is reading at an end of the kindergarten level between his decoding and comprehension skills. It is very probable at one point Child A was reading at a 2nd grade level, but due to the dyslexia has decreased in his ability.

Child A seemed to enjoy working on reading on the computer. Even though he was asked to do some activities that were difficult he cooperated every step of the way.

Child A struggles with being able to read sight words because he is not currently engaged in a reading program that focuses on them. He also struggles with reading words that do not fall into the closed pattern. Child A will benefit from a reading program that focuses on both sight words and phonics patterns along with reading lots of text.

Child A has been struggling with reading for a long time and his self-esteem has been affected as well. With Child A going to the 6th grade in the fall he will benefit from reading a lot of non-fiction text. This way he will not be reading books that seem to be too babyish for his intellect.

Some parents even use this report as a tool with the school system to get additional help for their child. This is fantastic. Once the classroom teacher sees the amount of information that the parent now has regarding their child, they become more empowered to be an advocate for the child.

Instructional Plan

On the assessment I don't go into huge details about what instruction I will be providing, but just the activities that will occur. Here is Child A's instructional plan.

Sight Words
Vowel Pattern Chart
Reading Practice and Comprehension with RAZ kids

That is it. It simply states the tools that the instructor will use. You don't have to go into detail on this part. The most important part is already in the parent's hand. The report identifies the problem and the solution.

Conclusion

This assessment is a peek into the amazing quality of services that you will be providing their child. Clearly, tutors that can come off in a knowledgeable, professional manner are going to be successful in their tutoring business and stand out against anyone else out there. Begin thinking how you can construct an assessment for the clients that you will be helping. This overall formula can be used for any subject.

12 Connecting with your students

Tutoring students online is only part of what you do to provide quality services. "Whatever you do, make sure you do it well," right? There is another component to your tutoring services that will make you stand out from the crowd, get you noticed, and get you more referrals.

What is that, you may be thinking. Well, it is authentically connecting with your students. Your students could be watching TV, playing with their friends, or doing anything else but hanging out with you on the computer. If you are not connecting with them, then they are not going to enjoy coming to their sessions and they are going to fight with their parents to begin their tutoring. When this kind of resistance exists, parents stop paying for the service. The worst part is the parent will most likely not tell you why they no longer need tutoring from you. They may make up an excuse about money or losing a job. In other words, they may lie about why they are stopping, rather than tell you the real problem.

I have found that I just don't always connect well with every kid, but I try every single day. In this chapter you are going to learn about the things that you can do to connect and engage with the students and the student's parents. You want both to be satisfied with the services you are providing them.

Tip #1 – If there is another kid or animal in the background, make note of it.

Personalize the time that you have with each of your students. Most likely you will be able to hear sounds in the background that will open the door for that child to connect with you. If you can hear the child's siblings in the background, ask them how old they are and what their names are. That way when they come up to the computer you can greet them by their names instead of referring to them as sister or brother. You can easily write this information on a document placed in the child's folder. That way, anytime you hear the brother in the background you can say something like, "Oh sounds like Joey is having a lot of fun today." That usually gets the child laughing or a little smile. You can generally use the expressions on your student's face to infer what kind of relationship he or she has with the sibling. That provides a good connection point and generates plenty of conversation.

I don't know of any kids that don't love their pets. If you hear that there is a dog in the background, then you can ask what kind of dog the child has. Ask the child the name of the pet and if you can't determine if it is a boy or a girl, then ask. That way when you hear Marley in the background you say something like, "Did you get to play with Marley today?"

Tip #2 – Tell your student that he or she is not allowed to smile.

Seriously, say this with the most sincere (not mean) tone that you can. Your student will begin laughing and smiling instantly. Then you follow it all up with, "Hey, I told you no smiling." This gets them in a good mood in no time.

If the parents can see that their child is smiling and having fun, even if the child didn't want to tutor, they feel like they are leaving their child in capable hands. At the end of the day, parents want their kids to have fun. If you can engage their child and make it fun for them, then they view the SERVICES that you are providing as a worthwhile investment.

Tip #3 – Smile

It is amazing how one little smile from you can spark a smile from the child. I love greeting the child with a smile. This is one of the reasons I tell them they can't smile if they are not smiling when we get onto the session together. This automatically changes the mindset of the child. If the child was having a bad day before, then this could change up everything for them.

I often have kids surprised that their time is up already after a half hour or hour. Most of the time it is because I try to make it as fun as I can.

Tip #4 – Give your student choices

Anytime that you can give a child choice, it results in a child that is more engaged than if you made all of the choices. My students who need to work on sight words are not allowed to make choices about doing that activity, but I have different background slides they can choose, and they love choosing what their background is going to be. Just this small bit of personalization makes the process enjoyable and memorable.

I always allow my students to choose the book that they want to read as well. I can even ask them why they chose the book. That will give me more information about the child to connect with them in the future.

Tip #5 – Ask your student about his/her day.

Every time I get on a new session with one of my students, I start it off by asking about their day. I usually get the very short response of, "Good." But I can probe deeper if time allows and say something like, "Tell me about your favorite thing that happened today." Another good one is, "Did you have a good lunch? What did you have?" I am usually asking these kinds of questions, listening to the response and opening up their materials. It is a great use of time.

Tip #6 – Be genuinely interested in what your student has to tell you.

At certain times your student is going to feel so comfortable with you that he or she will want to share stories with you. Listen with a genuine heart and then get back to the lesson. It usually only takes a minute or two for the child to share his or her excitement with you and this allows you to connect with him/her in a new way.

Kids love sharing information about the sports they are in. They want to share their victories with you because you are an important person to them.

These are all great ways to connect with the person on the other end. I do all of this during the lesson and keep my lessons to the time allotted. I am forced to because I have another student scheduled after them.

None of these ways of connecting with students takes a lot of time. The time that you invest in them will have big dividends for you. You will come off as personable and likeable. Guess what? People like to do business with people they like, know, and trust. So, give people a reason to like you by being the most authentic you that you can be. If any of the tips don't feel authentic to you, then try some other ways that fit your personality better. Trying to be someone that you are not will never make people feel authentically connected to you.

13 Good Communication

People who provide good services to their clients are good communicators. Neglecting to answer phone calls, respond to e-mail messages, or show up to a session are all signs of poor communication. If your communication skills are not clear, then you will have sales falling through the cracks of your business. This chapter is broken down into rules. These rules must be followed, or their will be consequences. In an online world, people seem to disappear into cyberspace. If you don't take these rules seriously, people won't refer you to others and they will eventually discontinue their services with you. They are also far more likely to leave a bad review.

Rule #1 Promptly return phone messages

Nothing proves your professionalism than responding to people in a quick manner. In this day and age, people expect other people to get back to them within 24 hours. If you wait days or weeks, then you can expect that they have already begun searching for someone else.

Rule #2 Listen to your customer

Your customer is going to reveal a lot about their preferred communication right from the start. People tend to use the type of communication they like to use best. So, if you are receiving emails from a client, most likely they prefer that method. If they send you texts, then they prefer that method. Whatever method you receive a message, respond in the same manner. If there is any question, ask them.

There are so many methods to reach out today that it is impossible for everyone to keep up with them. But here's the thing, if you expect your client to change their methods to communicate with you because you only use one type of communication, then this is going to lead to poor communication.

What would you expect to happen to a business that has poor communication? Clients become disgruntled. It closes down eventually or goes bankrupt, right? Well, the same thing can happen with your tutoring business.

I have to remember to keep my cell phone with me in my office because some clients will text me that they can't make a session. I have a 24-hour policy, but I also believe in flexibility. Sometimes parents just can't make it home in time and it is not my place to judge. I appreciate that people are trying to communicate with me, so I need to open myself up to listen to their form of communication.

Here are different communication forms to get familiar with.
Facebook messages
email
phone call
text
Zoom chat

Rule #3 Send a welcome packet in the mail stating all of the useful information they need to know

People appreciate being informed. Sending a welcome packet

in the mail vs. e-mail is going to do two things. First, it is going to get their attention more amongst all the noise of email and they will be more apt to read it. Second, it is going to show your professionalism. Sometimes emails don't have the same professional quality as a packet that arrives in the mail.

In the letter you can include
1. Why you are excited to work with them
2. Information about your cancellation policy
3. How often you will assess and give feedback
4. All of the ways that they can communicate with you
5. Payment plan
6. How to cancel services
7. How to put services on hold
8. How to reinstate services
9. How to leave a testimonial or recommendation
10. Thank them for the opportunity to work with their child

You might also want to inform them how to send you referrals. Referrals are one of the biggest ways that companies keep their business going. This is true in the online tutoring world as well. Just think of it, if each of your clients referred you to two people, you could stay in business off of referrals alone. In fact, many tutors do.

In the packet, you can even put a bookmark or something small that will give your new client some tips. Everybody loves free goodies.

Rule #4 – Create a schedule where you assess each of your students every 3 months.

Every 10 weeks the school system provides an overview of how a child is doing. They use the report card. In online tutoring, the parents are forking over their money and they want feedback as well.

However, the parents don't want general feedback like your child is getting much better in understanding what she is reading. They want details that back up how you know they are improving. So, reassess the child every 3 months and then report back to the parents regarding the results. The parents will be grateful that you did.

Rule #5 – Always communicate with your client when you need to cancel a session.

Sometimes things happen in life and you are not able to meet with a student at a certain time. Have blocks of time on your schedule available to do makeup sessions. Here is an example email of not being able to make a session.

Hi Angela,
I am so sorry, but I will not be able to tutor Brendon on Thursday night. My daughter is having her Christmas concert. I do have two other days that might work for you. One is Wednesday night at 7:00 pm and the other is Saturday morning at 10:00 am. Which time would work best for you?

I don't cancel a session often, but the beauty of having an online business is that it is pretty easy to switch things around. I love it. I don't even have to state the reason why I can't make the session. The important thing is that when I am not able to make a session, I tell them as early as I can, and I offer two other times that will work.

In conclusion, you want to be as clear in communication with each of your clients as you can, because at the end of the day this is what people who provide good service do. Remember to communicate with your client in the form of communication they like best and respond quickly. Send a welcome packet to their home that goes through all the details they need to know. Provide ongoing assessments and ongoing feedback to your clients regarding progress. Lastly, contact your clients through their favorite form of communication when you are not able to make a session. These tools are the basis of a good client relationship. Each of your clients deserves the VIP treatment, so give it to them.

14 Jumpstart Program

Throughout the book I have made reference to the Jumpstart Program. You may be wondering more about it and how it is different than the information that is provided in this book.

The program is not something that you mindlessly consume hoping it will get you results. I designed it so I can carefully guide you step by step. The assignments are chosen to ease you into actions that will expand your tutoring business. The best part that we take the journey as a group to get group synergy going. Group momentum will inspire and motivate you to take actions. It is amazing.

I also assign you to a team and a coach so that you can begin making connections with other tutors. Many tutors don't realize this, but other tutors make great referral partners. Few tutors like referring people they don't know. But working together as a team begins to create camaraderie. Soon trust builds. In the course of the Jumpstart program, participants will begin building relationships of trust with other tutors.

The goal of the course is to help you get one student or a whole lot more so that you can experience more lightbulb moments from your students. In fact, I want you to get so many students that you light up and entire city. Top tutors get 10-25 students every time I open the 10-week course. Imagine having a fully booked business in 3 months' time. It is possible and has happened several times.

If you are the type of person that does well with specific steps to put into place at the right moment, then this will be perfect for you. This program only opens a few times throughout the year, but you can always reserve your seat. **Get on the Waiting List for the Jumpstart Program** [29]

I have personally found I accomplish a lot more when I am taking a class or course than when I am not. I feel like I have direction, so I act on the things that I am learning. When I am not part of a class, I sometimes can fall into the mode of telling myself I will do it later. Then later never comes because I make excuses to not follow through on it again. Accountability is huge for me and when I take a class and doing the activities it always has a huge impact on me and my business.

Here is what a couple of the students that went through the Jumpstart Program had to say about their experience.

It has been a lovely experience working with Joanne. I found her through the internet, and I mailed her one day with no hope of my mail being answered. And guess what? She replied to my mail in less than 24 hours with each point covered in depth. She pointed out where I was going wrong and motivated me to not give up. After that there has been no looking back. I took her Jumpstart Program where she systematically shows us what to do. She starts with mindset and guides us into positive thinking. Then she leads us through how to strategize, organize and market our business.

Joanne is always there for you and supports you in your greatest time of need. She is an amazing business coach. Quite honestly, I consider myself very lucky to have her in my life. Life without her would be very difficult. I operate from Mumbai, India and I currently work with 20 students from all over the globe. Undoubtedly, she is the pillar of my success.

Sandhya Bajaj

Another client of the Jumpstart Program raved about her experience as well.

Before working with Joanne and the Jumpstart Program, I had about 5 students and wasn't getting paid enough. I had started my tutoring business about a year before. I loved what I did but I knew I wasn't really making money at it. I knew I had to get more students and/or charge more.
In addition, I felt unorganized and overwhelmed. How could I possibly tutor more students? I was driving to my client's houses. I would drive as far as 70 miles round trip. I was only getting paid enough to cover costs, if that.

During the program, I focused on developing my online presence, getting organized using Joanne's systems, and getting my name out there in my community. I toyed with the idea of tutoring online and even advertised that I tutored online, on my website. I still wasn't fully convinced it would be best for the kids I tutored. Besides I was afraid my technical skills would cause too many issues. I did get some new students during the course and I did manage to raise my price. It actually took me several months to fully implement all that

I learned from the Jumpstart course. It especially took a while to fully embrace the idea of tutoring online.

As a result of the program, and the pain of having my clients miss tutoring when I travelled, I have finally transitioned all of my students but one to online tutoring. Even though it took some time to get here, I would not go back! Kids are able to meet with me more often. I can travel without clients missing their tutoring sessions. I have gained confidence to the place where I am charging what I need to make money. The majority of my clients are set up to pay monthly, automatically, via PayPal. What a huge time saver! I now have 9 students and make $1200 a month putting in less time than I was before the Jumpstart Program. The best part, I feel relaxed and in control. With the systems I have put in place because of the program I feel I could easily take on several more students and still be relaxed. I love my job!!

Laura Kulp

15 What Your Life Could Look Like

As you have been reading this book, you are probably one of two types of people. You are either someone who has already started your own tutoring company at home and are looking for new strategies and ideas, or you are thinking of becoming an online tutor. Either way, congratulations for being a part of this journey.

Online tutoring is a new career path that didn't exist when any of us were children. We are on the cutting edge of technology, and it is an exciting place to be.

Recently I had a 3rd grade student with dyslexia begin to make major growth. She had made slow progress, but all of a sudden it has all started to click for her. She is beginning to see patterns and she is reading words that once she wouldn't even attempt. The feeling that I had in my heart was priceless. Seriously, I felt like I was walking on cloud nine.

To know that I have made a difference for this child in ways that other educators couldn't is the most priceless gift that I could receive. I receive this gift on a daily basis and you will get to receive this gift as well.

Most likely you became a teacher or a tutor for reasons just like this, right? As soon as I had my own children though, there was a big hole in my life. I love my kids more than anything in the world and I was sacrificing that to be of service to other people's kids in the classroom. Now I have the best of both worlds. Supermom by day, Super Tutor by night and it is all from the comfort of my home.

There couldn't be a more glorious lifestyle. I can travel the world whenever I want. I don't have to wait for when I have time off from school, which happens to be the busy season for traveling. I can travel to awesome places on the off season and enjoy them without all of the hustle and bustle. I can bring my tutoring company wherever I go. I have the ultimate in flexibility. If I want to take a week off, I just let my clients know. We work it out. There are times like when I took my family to Disney World for Mickey's Spectacular Halloween event, and I just wanted to focus on my family. So, I did. I added sessions in during the month to make up for the time that would be lost. It was wonderful.

I went to the beach in the winter when it is super cold here in Wisconsin and worked a few hours during the day and enjoyed the rest of the time at the beach in San Diego. I got to visit the zoo, go to Sea World, and just soak in the rays. It was awesome.

I get to be home for my kids on the first day of school every single year, without having to ask someone if I can.

I took my whole family to China and experienced the world in ways I never thought possible.

I took my kids to Disney world in Hong Kong.

We've gotten to experience toilets that we had no idea even how to use. Those of you that have been to China know what I mean.

I got to be room mom and volunteer in my daughters' schools when they were younger.

I am a #1 top selling author on Amazon for <u>31 Days to Become a Better Reader: Increasing your Struggling Reader's Reading Level</u>[30] all because I have time to write about my passions.

I have spoken at schools and motivated kids to read, write, and illustrate. The picture below shows me talking to a group of 4th graders about my book <u>Three Little Sisters Learn to Get Along</u>[31].

I am living a life I couldn't even have dreamed of as a child. Now, I know that my dream life is not what your dream life looks like or what you may want it to look like. We are all different right? So, this book isn't going to end with my story. It is going to end with yours. I want you to think about what your dreams are. What do you want to accomplish, how much money do you want to make, where are places that you want to go, who do you want to inspire? Do you want to do this with time freedom, financial freedom, and complete flexibility? Then make that part of your story. You can be, do, and have, whatever your heart desires. If you can think it, then you can achieve it. Don't let people who aren't living their dreams sidetrack you from living yours. Teachers have been locked up in classrooms for too long. It is time to break free, do what you love, and get paid what your worth.

Dream big. What will your story be?

16 Now What?

"Happiness is not something that you get once you are successful. Success is a direct result of being happy."

If you are like me, then you don't want this journey that we have had together to end. There is so much more that I want to be able to teach you so that you can be recession, pandemic and competition proof, doing what you love doing.

I mentioned earlier that I have created a community of people that want to support you in your journey. If you decide to join us, then go the Ultimate Support Group for Online Tutors on Facebook. Let us stand out as the best tutors all over the world that are the most highly sought out group of educators.

I am sure that people have told you your whole life that teachers don't make a 6-figure income. Well, they don't make it because nobody has ever believed that they can. We are starting a new era here. Without teachers we wouldn't have doctors, lawyers, or presidents. So, let's continue making a difference in the lives of others and in our own lives as well.

ABOUT THE AUTHOR

Joanne Kaminski is #1 top selling author and recipient of the S.T.A.R. award for her book *31 Days to Become a Better Reader: Increasing your Struggling Reader's Reading Level*. She has also written *Three Little Sisters Learn to Get Along* and *How to Raise Non-fiction Reading Levels*. She has been an online reading tutor since 2010 and is able to close the reading gap a full year with just 8-12 hours of instruction.

Joanne is currently teaching kids online, but also teaching teachers how to increase or replace their current income by becoming an online tutor in whatever area of teaching they love the most. Not only are teachers and tutors able to learn more about this career choice than has ever been available to them before but they are also receiving support every step of the way.

Joanne works with tutors that are great tutors but lack the know-how to market themselves all over the world to get students. Most tutors that work with her make 4-5 figures a month doing what they love.

As a mom, wife, friend, and daughter, Joanne has realized that too much of our time is spent being concerned about the wrong things. Being of service to her family, friends, students, and other teachers gives her a sense of purpose.

Endnotes

---

[1] https://www.grandviewresearch.com/industry-analysis/online-tutoring-services-market

[2] Fountas, Irene C. and Pinnell, Gay Su. Leveled Literacy Intervention System. Portsmouth NH: Heinemann Publishing www.forntasandpinnel.com

[3] Dyer, Wayne (2010). The Shift: Taking your Life from Ambition to Meaning. United States, Hay House Inc.

[4] Byrnes, Rhonda (2006). The Secret. New York: Beyond Words Publishing.

[5] Schafer, Fred (2013). How to Make Great Things Happen in Your Life. Australia: Condor Books.

[6] Byrnes, Rhonda (2006). The Secret. New York: Beyond Words Publishing.

[7] Women Leading from the Soul Conference March 5, 2013.

[8] Parker, S.L. (2005). 212° the Extra Degree. Flower Mound, TX: The Walk the Talk Company.

[9] www.ted.com

[10] Byrnes, Rhonda (2006). The Secret. New York: Beyond Words Publishing.

[11] Dyer, Wayne (2012). Wishes Fulfilled: Mastering the Art of Manifesting. New York: Hay House Publishing.

[12] Hill, Napoleon (2009). Think and Grow Rich. United States: White Dog

[13] Covey, Stephen (2012). The Seven Habits of Highly Effective People. New York: Rosetta Books.

[14] Kiyosaki, Robert (1998). Rich Dad, Poor Dad: What the Rich Teach their Children and the Poor and Middle Class do not! New York: Warner Books Inc.

[15] Tolle, Eckhart (1999). The Power of Now. Novato, CA: Namaste

Publishing.

[16] Darren Hardy. (2020). *Compound Effect.* Paris: Hachette Go.

[17] Hicks, Esther (2006). The Law of Attraction. Carlsbad, CA: Hay House Publishing.

[18] Canfield, Jack (2010). Chicken Soup for the Soul: Think Positive. United States: Chicken Soup for the Soul Publishing, LLC.

[19] www.flylady.net

[20] Byrnes, Rhonda (2010). The Power. New York: Atria Books

[21] Jumpstart Your Online Tutoring Business Masterclass. This course opens a few times a year. This video has details. https://www.onlinetutorcoach.com/Jump-In-100

[22] LastPass password manager and vault app https://www.lastpass.com

[23] www.tutorbird.com

[24] https://www.facebook.com/groups/303391446535402/

[25] www.wisestamp.com

[26] www.wix.com

[27] http://www.sparkol.com

[28] Iny, Dany. (2011) Engagement from Scratch! How Super-Community Builders Create a Loyal Audience and How You Can Do the Same! Available on Amazon

[29]thttps://www.onlinetutorcoach.com/waiting-list-for-jumpstart

[30] Kaminski, Joanne (2012). 31 Days to Become a Better Reader: Increasing Your Struggling Reader's Reading Level. United States. Available on Amazon

[31] Kaminski, Joanne (2013). Three Little Sisters Learn to Get Along. Available on Amazon

Printed in Great Britain
by Amazon

42797731R00079